Sabbatarian

CONCORDANCE

AND

COMMENTARY

BY

GERALD N. WRIGHT

ISBN 0-933672-35-7
Star Catalog #C-1572
Published by
Star Bible Publications, Inc.
410 N. Dove, Grapevine, TX 76051
P.O.Box 821220,Fort Worth, TX 76182
CALL 1-800 433-7507 or 817 416-5889 CST

DEDICATED TO
MY
FATHER & MOTHER
MR. & MRS. HAROLD B. WRIGHT

—CONTENTS—

INTRODUCTION

Have you ever gotten into a discussion with a proponent of the sabbath and found yourself without an answer to one of his "unheard of" proof texts? Well, I have, and it was then that I wished I had memorized all the comments on such passages as found in the many good books written on the subject of Sabbatarianism. Indeed books written on Sabbatarianism are legion. and the many so-called "iron-clad arguments" in favor of sabbath-keeping have been refuted in a multitude of ways. Yet the average Bible student (as most of us are) does not have the time to memorize all these books in order to be capable of meeting every argument. Thus wouldn't it be helpful if a book existed which contained every proof-passage (sabbath or Decalogue) in chronological order—Genesis through Revelation—with a compilation of the many comments from other books in condensed form? Surely it would!

This book was put together with such in mind—to be a handy pocket guide.

Due to the nature of this book, being a chronological concordance of compiled thoughts, this writer offers little new or original information on the subject of Sabbatarianism. Yet, due to its comprehensiveness and chronological style, offering finger-tip accessibility to every (hopefully) passage concerning the sabbath argument, this writer believes this book will serve well as a valuable tool in studying, discussing and even debating the subject. The reader will notice that I have not included the specific reference in footnotes for each comment borrowed from another source, lest the simplicity and comprehension of this publication be hampered by a multitude of footnotes. The reader is therefore asked to look to the Bibliography for the various sources considered in writing this book. I thank each author contributing to this work.

Special Note: If the reader knows of other Sabbatarian proof texts which are not found in this book, then this author would appreciate it if such were forwarded to him (via the publisher). Such will be researched and included in any later reprints.

Abbreviations: KJV - King James Version; ASV - American Standard Version; RSV - Revised Standard Version; NASV - NEW American Standard Version; NEB - New English Bible. The ASV will be used in all quotations in this book.

SEE INDEX FOR ALL PASSAGES
COVERED IN THIS BOOK

GENESIS

Genesis 2:2f "And on the seventh day God finished his work which he had made; and he rested on the seventh day from all his work which he had made. And God blessed the seventh day, and hallowed it; because that in it he rested from all his work which God had created and made." ASV

ASSERTIONS

One: God's resting on the seventh day set it apart as a holy day from the very beginning, as God's sabbath day, for all men to keep.

Two: When God blesses something, it is blessed forever (cf Numbers 23:20; I Chronicles 17:27).

Three: Adam kept the sabbath.

Four: Adam had to keep the sabbath, for he kept all the ten commandments. Paul confirmed this by stating that without the ten commandments there would be no sin; yet Adam sinned; thus he broke the ten commandments (Romans 5:12-14).

Five: Ancient historians also bear witness to the fact that all nations (not just the Jews) have kept the sabbath at times (See Josephus, Against Apion, Bk.II-40).

ANSWERS

One: God's resting on the seventh day did not make it holy, nor did his resting on it set it apart as the "sabbath day" to be kept by man.

1. Genesis 2:2f does not say God kept or created the sabbath by resting on the seventh day; it simply says God "rested" (not the word sabbath in any form) or ceased from creating on the seventh day. (Such is pure-

ly an anthropomorphism, for God needs no rest - Isaiah 40:28; John 5:17.) There is no mention whatsoever of the word "sabbath" in this text. In fact, the word sabbath is purely a Hebrew word, always referring to the Jewish rest days, never appearing in the book of Genesis, and first appearing in the Old Testament in Exodus 16:23 — about 2500 years after God rested! (The Hebrew "shabath" is better translated "rest" than Sabbath.)

2. If God's resting on the seventh day automatically sanctified the particular period he rested upon, then those who would keep the sabbath would have to keep the specific hours God rested, for the very hours would be holy. (a) Such is impossible because there's no way of determining exactly when such would be on our clocks and calendars. Actually, it is difficult to determine the precise hours God rested on in Genesis 2:2f. For it is quite likely that he did not rest as the Jews later did — from evening to evening (Leviticus 23:32; cf Mark 15:42) — but rather from morning to morning (Genesis 1:31 —2:3; cf Keil & Delitzsch, "The Pentateuch." Vol. I, Genesis 1:2-5.) (b) Such is impossible on a round earth. For some on one side of the globe would be keeping Sabbath on the seventh day, while others on the other side of the globe, in order to keep the Sabbath at the same time as God did (indeed He only rested on one seventh-day period) and as those on the other side, would be keeping Sabbath on Friday or Sunday, depending on which side of the globe one chose as having the seventh day coinciding with God's seventh day—whether behind or ahead of the other side of the globe in time! Actually, only one side of the globe could ever keep Sabbath correctly. Also, in our modern jet age, one could skip keeping the Sabbath altogether (just fly across the time zone) or keep it twice every week!

3. The seventh day became a holy day—the Sabbath day—not because God rested on it, nor even because he blessed

it, but because he "hallowed" it, meaning to set apart for religious observance (Genesis 2:3). It had to be made holy (See Mark 2:23-28). This fact is further made evident when we look at other days which became sacred sabbaths, just as holy as the seventh-day Sabbath, yet days on which God had not rested at all. He just sanctified them (cf Leviticus 23:27-32).

4. Genesis 2:3 does not say when the seventh day was "hallowed"; it just says it was the day God chose to hallow because he had rested (past tense) in it. Thus God sanctified the seventh day as a holy day some time after he rested on it. (a) It is obvious, due to the total absence of the word sabbath in the Bible or religious history for the first 2500 years of time, that God did not hallow it immediately when he rested. (b) The seventh day is first recorded as being hallowed in the book of Exodus and not before (cf Exodus 16:23: 20:11). (c) In Genesis 2:3 we have a typical example of the use of prolepsis in writing (the representation of a future act as if already accomplished). Since Moses wrote the book of Genesis some 2500 years after the creation and also after the seventh day had been hallowed at Sinai, he recorded the two events (God's resting on the seventh day and his hallowing it) since related, in the same context, though occurring at different times. Some other examples of prolepsis are found in: Genesis 2:14; 3:20 — where Eve was called the mother of all living before she was the mother of anyone; Genesis 4:20; I Samuel 4:1 with 7:12; Matthew 10:4; etc. By way of illustration, we say President Lincoln was born in Kentucky when he was not a **President** at the time of his birth.

Two: This text does not say God's blessing the sabbath meant the sabbath would last eternally.

1. God's blessing something has nothing to do with its permanency, nor are his blessings to be thought of as irrevocable. God can remove his blessings to serve his purposes or when those blessed become no longer de-

servant of such (See Deuteronomy 28-30 "The Covenant of Blessings and Cursings").

2. Numbers 23:20 has nothing to do with the blessing of the sabbath day. It rather deals with God's pronounced blessing upon Israel. Also, this text doesn't say **God couldn't** reverse his blessing (as he later did curse Israel) but **Balaam couldn't** reverse it.

3. I Chronicles 17:27 has nothing to do with God's blessing the sabbath either. It concerns itself with God's blessing David's house and nothing more (See Exodus 31: 17f —One, on the word "forever").

Three: Adam did not keep the Sabbath.

1. Nowhere does it say Adam kept the sabbath (especially since the word sabbath does not appear in the entire book of Genesis), nor is there one reference to his observing any sabbath function, regulation, punishment, etc. To say Adam kept the sabbath is pure assumption.

2. To say Adam kept the sabbath is to have the pattern of sabbath-keeping (six days of work and then a day of rest on the seventh - Exodus 20:9) broken from the very outset. For, if Adam rested on the first sabbath (the one on which God rested at the close of creation), then he rested on his second day (not seventh), for he had only been created the day before! Thus he had not yet worked six days. He broke the pattern from the beginning!

3. Ancient scholars, many with accurate knowledge of Jewish beliefs and traditions concerning the keeping of the sabbath, deny that Adam, Abraham or anyone before Sinai kept the sabbath (Justin Martyr, "Dialogue with Trypho," ch. 19; Irenaeus, Adv. Hoeres, lib. 4, c 30; Tertulian, "Against the Jews," section 4; Eusebius, Eccl. Hist., Bk. 1, Ch. 4).

4. It would not matter if it could be proven that Adam kept the sabbath (which it cannot), as well as all the

godly men who lived after him until the cross of Christ, such would still not mean Christians under Christ's new covenant are bound to keep it. Christians do not have to follow in the steps of Adam, but Christ (See I Corinthians 9:21). Adam and his family had to offer up animal sacrifices, but we do not have to do the same (Genesis 4:4f).

Four: Adam did not keep the ten commandments as a codified system, the Decalogue, including the fourth command, the sabbath. And such is not necessary for sin to exist.

1. The ten commandments did not exist as a codified system of law until Sinai - 2500 years after Adam was created. (a) We've already seen that the word sabbath, much less the sabbath command, does not appear until Sinai. Thus the **ten** commandments could not have been kept by Adam by reason of the absence of one of the ten, number four! (b) No copy of the Decalogue — a complete and chronological list of the ten commandments — has ever been found before Sinai. (c) The Bible declares that the ten commandments did not exist until Sinai (Deuteronomy 5:1-3: Galatians 3:17).

2. One can sin without breaking one of the ten commandments. (a) See comments on Romans 4:15; 5:12 for the Sabbatarian assumptions there. (b) Adam, as his posterity, had many commandments to keep which are not found in the Decalogue, of which the violation of any one of them would have constituted sin (Genesis 2:17 - not eat of the tree of knowledge of good and evil; Genesis 4:3 with I John 3:12-Note that Cain's sin was of a ceremonial law!; cf Genesis 26:5; I John 3:4). One doesn't need to break any specific law to sin; he can just violate his conscience or fail to do something good (Romans 14:23; James 4:17). No doubt, Adam was aware of the high moral principles of God (nine of the ten commandmenats are inherently moral; the sabbath

is not - See Exodus 20:8-11). Yet he was motivated unto keeping such out of higher ideals than a codified list, i.e., out of love for God and neighbor (See I Timothy 1:8f). Thus to say that the only way one can sin is to break one of the written commandments found in the Decalogue is false. (c) To say that every command of God and transgression of man is actually related to one of the ten commandments, as Sabbatarians do, is to beg the issue and raise the question as to which law was added at Sinai if all laws are but clarifications of, or ammendments to, the Decalogue (Galatians 3:19). Note: Sabbatarians say the eating of the forbidden fruit (Genesis 2:17) is the breaking of the eighth commandment not to steal or the sixth not to kill - bringing death upon all men in so doing.

3. It would not matter if one could prove that Adam kept the ten commandments, for such still does not mean the Christian must keep them all, especially since the Decalogue was abolished as a system of law at the cross, and especially since the sabbath command was specifically pointed out as not a part of the new covenant (II Corinthians 3:6ff; Colossians 2:14-17).

Five: Ancient historians do not validate sabbath-keeping before and apart from the Sinaitic covenant.

1. See comments of the scholars at references listed at Three-3; also Revelation 1:10.

2. Josephus (Against Apion, B. II, 40) says the pagan nations who kept the sabbath did so in immitation of the Jews. Thus this does not substantiate the claim that men knew to keep the sabbath by some God-given intuition in all nations, nor does it support the claim that all nations kept it before or apart from the Sinaitic covenant. The only ones who kept it were those who kept it through association with those who kept the Sinaitic covenant, the Jews.

3. Though ancient historians can be alluded to in support of Biblical fact, they, alone, cannot be used as authority in religion. Thus the Sabbatarian is still bound to supply scriptural testimony in support of his claims. Such he has never been able to do.

Genesis 26:5 "Because that Abraham obeyed my voice, and kept my charge, my commandments, my statutes, and my laws."

ASSERTION: Abraham kept the ten commandments, including the sabbath command.

ANSWER: It is pure assumption to say Abraham kept the **ten** commandments when the word "ten" is not in the text.

1. There are over 800 texts containing the words "the commandments," and about 49 out of 50 of them refer to something more or less than the entire Decalogue.

2. All that God told Abraham to do can be considered as commandments: his leaving his country (Genesis 12:1); his going to sacrifice Isaac (Ibid. 22:1ff; cf Exodus 8:27); his going in unto Sarah to father a child (Genesis 15:3-6); his circumcising all the males (Ibid.17:10ff); and any other time he "obeyed" God's voice (26:5 cf Hebrews 11:8ff).

3. Notice that Abraham also kept the "statutes and laws" (Genesis 26:5). Now, if the mention of Abraham's keeping "commandments" means he kept the ten commandment covenant, then the mention of his keeping "statutes and laws" means he also kept the ceremonial law of Moses, for Sabbatarians say such terms refer to those ceremonial laws written by Moses in the book of the law. Thus now I am really interested in knowing which law was added 400 years after Abraham at Sinai if he was already keeping the ten commandment laws and the so-called ceremonial laws of Moses (Galatians 3:16f)!

4. This occasion transpired over 400 years before the ten commandment covenant was first given (Galatians 3:16f) and when the **fathers** (Abraham was one of the fathers) were not under it (Deuteronomy 1:8; 5:3)!

5. Again it must be stated that what men did or were told to do before the cross of Christ and the ratification of his new covenant has no bearing on what Christians must do. Thus it does not matter what commandments Abraham kept (as he kept the commandment of circumcision and we do not), such still does not mean we must keep the same.

EXODUS

Exodus 12:11-14 "It is Jehovah's passover. .ye shall keep it a feast by an ordinance forever"

GOOD POINTS

One: Just because some thing or day is called the "Lord's" (his by virtue of his creation of it, establishing it, ordaining it to be, etc.) does not mean it can't later be done away with. This is one of the arguments used by Sabbatarians at Mark 2:28.

Two: The fact that something is said to be kept "forever" does not necessarily mean as long as time exists. For the Old Testament Passover was abolished with the rest of the old covenant ceremonies and replaced with our Passover, even Christ (I Corinthians 5:7).

Exodus 16:23-30 "And he said unto them, This is that which Jehovah hath spoken, Tomorrow is a solemn rest, a holy sabbath unto Jehovah. . V.26 Six days ye shall gather it (manna); but on the seventh day is the sabbath, in it there shall be none. V.27 And it came to pass on the seventh day, that there went out some of the people to gather, and they found none. V.28 And Jehovah said unto Moses, How long refuse ye to keep my commandments and my laws? V.29 See, for that Jehovah hath given you the sabbath, therefore he giveth you on the sixth day the bread of two days; abide ye every man in his place, let no man go out of his place on the sabbath day. V.30 So the people rested on the seventh day."

ASSERTIONS

One: This shows the Sabbath was in existence before the giving of the law of Moses at Sinai (Exodus 19-20)

Two: This shows the sabbath had been a command long before this occasion, even while in Egyptian bondage, for they were rebuked for failing to keep it, along with the other commandments, for some time by that time: "**How long refuse ye to keep** my commandments and laws?" (V.28).

ANSWERS

One: The sabbath being instituted before the Sinaitic covenant.

1. This was in anticipation of the covenant God was about to make with Israel at Sinai, even as the Lord's Supper was introduced before the establishment of the new covenant and its being a part of it (Matthew 26:28; cf Hebrews 9:15ff).

2. This external observance (the sabbath) was so chosen by God at this point to see—"prove"—if the Israelites would walk in the law he would give them at Sinai (Exodus 16:4). If they were already keeping the sabbath command, then their further keeping it wouldn't have

proved anything which had not already been proven or disproven.

Two: There is no indication in this context that the sabbath command had been given before this occasion or known and neglected before this by the Jews.

1. Where does it say the words "How long refuse ye" extend back into Egyptian bondage? It doesn't say any such thing. To say so is pure assumption. All the indications in the Exodus account point to their rebellion (refusing to walk by God's commands) which commenced with their exit from Egypt and not before (See Exodus 14:11f; 15:24ff; 16:2f,27). This agrees with all the other accounts which say the covenant, including the sabbath, was given to Israel after their departure from Egyptian bondage (See at Deuteronomy 5:1-15). Also, if their refusal to keep the **commandments** at this point means they had been under the **ten** commandments all along, even in Egypt, then they were also under the ceremonial laws, for this text says they had also been refusing to keep the "laws" (V. 28 - commandments, according to Sabbatarians, means the ten commandments; laws means the Mosaical laws). If this be so, then again I must ask which law was added at Sinai? For the Jews were already keeping both the moral laws of God and the so-called ceremonial laws of Moses (Galatians 3:19)

2. There are many statements and facts in Exodus sixteen which prove this was the initial giving of the sabbath and that the Jews were in no way familiar with its observance. (a) This was a revelation and not a reminder:"This is that which Jehovah hath spoken" (V.23). (b) They were not used to keeping the sabbath regulations e.g., not to go out and to rest: "On the seventh day, then there went out some of the people" (V. 27; cf Numbers 15:32ff). (c) Some of the regulations of this

initial sabbath were later suspended, as the abiding in doors was not mandatory in Canaan (V.29). This shows this was an initial sabbath in its preparatory stages. This also shows the Lord can regulate the sabbath, even abolish it (cf Mark 2:28: Colossians 2:14-17).

3. This text further shows that the sabbath was given only to the Jews: "Jehovah hath given **you** the sabbath" (V.29, cf V. 1 where Israel is the "you" under discussion; See Exodus 31:13-17).

Exodus 19:5-8 "Keep my (God's) covenant...V8 And all the people answered together, and said, All that Jehovah hath spoken we will do. And Moses reported the words of the people unto Jehovah."

COMMENT: Sabbatarians seek to prove two covenants are under consideration here — God's covenant "my covenant" (V.5) and the people's covenant, i.e., their agreement to keep God's covenant (V.8). See Exodus 24:7f and Deuteronomy 31:24-26 to refute such a notion.

Exodus 20:8-11 "Remember the sabbath day, to keep it holy. V.9 Six days shalt thou labor, and do all thy work; V.10 but the seventh day is a sabbath unto Jehovah thy God (the seventh day is the sabbath of the Lord KJV). V.11 for in six days Jehovah made heaven and earth, the sea, and all that in them is, and rested the seventh day: wherefore Jehovah blessed the sabbath day, and hallowed it."

ASSERTIONS

One: This is not the giving of a new command, the sabbath command, but the restating of one they had failed to keep — "remember" — in the past. (One **remembers** the past and not the present or future!)

Two: The sabbath is Jehovah's sabbath and not the Jews' as many teach.

Three: The fourth command is the only one which shows God to be the giver of the Decalogue.

ANSWERS

One: Concerning the word "remember"

1. If it is used in reference to the past, then the farthest in the past one can scripturally go and find a sabbath command, regulation, etc., is Exodus 16:23! We find no account in all the book of Genesis of God sanctifying the sabbath, giving regulations concerning the sabbath, punishing violators of it, etc., (See Genesis 2:2f-prolepsis explained), and we find no record of anyone keeping it so it could be remembered by others (in the future) as once being kept (in the past). The Biblical record gives us every reason to believe the sabbath was first hallowed after the Exodus from Egypt (Exodus 16:23; 20:11). Also, the same is true concerning the giving of the Decalogue in which the sabbath command is found (See Deuteronomy 5:1-15).

2. The word "remember" was also used in charging people to remember in the future what was then being commanded (Exodus 13:3). Thus their statement that one only remembers the past is incorrect.

Two: "Jehovah's sabbath" (sabbath of the Lord - KJV) proves nothing as far as who was obligated to keep it (what nation) or as to how long it would endure as a commandment.

1. The Passover was also called "Jehovah's Passover," and even Sabbatarians admit it was only given to the Jews and was abolished at the cross (Exodus 12:11). The Passover, though called the Lord's, was also called the feast of the Jews (John 6:4). Thus something can be called Jehovah's and still pertain only to a particular

group of people. By the way, the sabbath was also called Israel's sabbath — "her sabbaths" (Hosea 2.11). Thus the sabbath was the Jews' sabbath.

2. Actually, emphasizing the authorship – "of the Lord" – of the sabbath here further proves that sabbath-keeping was not an intrinsic, already historic moral principle and practice, and that God had to personally and specifically sanctify it by command in order for it to be equally and perpetually binding along with the other nine historical moral principles of the Decalogue. And without such specific dictums from God setting certain days apart from and above other normal days, there is absolutely nothing "moral" about keeping certain days: they are all otherwise equal and morally neutral (Romans 14:5; Galatians 4:10; See Mark 2:23–28). By way of illustration, a person on a desert island can always know -- simply by using his trained conscience (by God's word) — if and when he violates typical, historical moral laws of God: if he has stolen, murdered, etc. For such are always wrong, every day. Yet the sabbath command is unique, being the only one of the Ten governed by time, and that same person could not know--without time-keeping records and devices--if he had rested on the right day or not (See Genesis 2:2f, One). And it would be immoral to condemn a person for violating something he had no possibility of knowing for sure if he was right or wrong! So the keeping of any certain period of time as a moral requirement must be understood in the context of revealed, regulated, religious environment (Israel's) and not as common, intrinsically moral, universal law. God never commanded all men to keep sabbath. (Such is why the Gentiles didn't!) He never commanded Christians to keep it. His only specific sabbath command to them is to allow no one--Jew or Sabbatarian– to bind it on them (Colossians 2:16)!

3. If the seventh day, as per this text (Exodus 20:10), is unalterable, then why do Sabbatarians do some acts

of labor on the sabbath contrary to the instructions of this very text? They will tell you that such ceremonial aspects of keeping the sabbath were abolished at the cross. Well, if such be so, then why do they forbid certain types of physical labors on the sabbath day? Where in the New Testament, after the abolishment of the ceremonial regulations at the cross, do they find their prohibitions concerning working on the sabbath, specifically speaking that is? They cannot show one positive, specific, sabbath regulation after the cross; nor can they show where the specific regulation concerning the building of a fire on the sabbath was specifically abolished (Exodus 35:3). Thus they do not keep Jehovah's sabbath, not according to any testament!

Three: God announced his authorship before the first commandment (V.2), as one does not usually wait until the middle of a presentation to declare his authorship. His name also appears in the third commandment (V.7).

Exodus 23:10f — The seventh year sabbath (cf Leviticus 25:4).

Exodus 23:12 "Six days thou shalt do thy work, and on the seventh day thou shalt rest; that thine ox and thine ass may have rest, and the son of thy handmaid, and the sojourner, may be refreshed."

ASSERTION: This passage shows that the Gentiles - "sojourners" — kept the sabbath.

ANSWER: This passage does not say the "sojourners" kept the sabbath.

1. This says the Israelites — "**thou** shalt rest" (cf 20:2)— were to keep the sabbath in order also that others might be refreshed, including even the beasts. The Israelites held strangers to hard service, and they needed the respite resultant of the Jews' resting. Yet this does not

mean they kept the sabbath as a religious observance, anymore than did the beasts keep it!

2. The only Gentiles ("sojourners") who had to keep the many laws and regulations of the Jews were those residing amongst the people of Israel, those within the gates, proselytes, visitors, etc. (Exodus 12:48; Leviticus 16:29; 17:8,10,12; 18:26; 19:33; 20:2; 25:45; Numbers 9:14; 15:14f,26,29; Deuteronomy 5:14; Isaiah 56:1-8). Thus this has nothing to do with what the common Gentile outside of Israel did.

Exodus 24:7f "And he took the book of the covenant, and read in the audience of the people: and they said, All that Jehovah hath spoken will we do, and be obedient. And Moses took the blood, and sprinkled it on the people, and said, Behold the blood of the covenant, which Jehovah hath made with you concerning all these words."

ASSERTIONS

One: The "book of the covenant" is not the Decalogue; it is only the words of Moses. The book was that placed **outside** the ark (Deuteronomy 31:26), while the Decalogue was that placed **inside** the ark (Ibid. 10:5). Thus this was the people's covenant to keep the Decalogue (Exodus 19:5-8).

Two: The blood ratified the Mosaical code and the people's covenant and not the Decalogue covenant.

ANSWERS

One: The "book of the covenant" included the Decalogue.

1. The book outside the ark included the Decalogue (See Deuteronomy 31:24-26).

2. The only covenant mentioned from Exodus 19:5 through 24:8 is the ten commandment covenant, including

all the by-laws, ordinances, statutes, and laws connected with it. Only one covenant was made at Sinai (Deuteronomy 29:1), the ten commandment covenant (Exodus 34:28), and it contained ordinances (not just moral commandments), statutes, and laws (Hebrews 9:1-4).

3. This covenant is "the covenant" which included "all the words" which "Jehovah had spoken unto them." **Before** the words were spoken the people agreed to keep them (Exodus 19:8). **After** the words were spoken the people reconfirmed their agreement to keep them (Ibid. 24:7f). Now the words spoken **inbetween** these two agreements included the ten commandments: "God spake all these words, saying. . .Thou shalt have no other gods before me. . ."(Ibid. 20:1ff). These words were also written in the book of the covenant, making up "all" the words of Jehovah. None were left out by Moses (as the Decalogue) when he read from the book!

4. This covenant is the one which Jehovah made with them—"Jehovah made with you"—and not some so-called people's covenant to keep God's covenant (24:8). Such a "people's covenant," separate and apart from the Decalogue covenant, does not exist. The people's agreement to keep God's covenant does not constitute a separate covenant. Normal covenants have conditions to be met by both parties (except for unconditional promises —Galatians 3:16-18), and the people's agreement to keep God's laws was only their keeping their part (of second party) of the Sinaitic covenant (See also Hebrews 8:6-13; 9:15-17).

Two: This ratification with the blood was of the entire Sinaitic covenant, including the Decalogue and all the laws given through Moses.

1. If this wasn't the ratification of the Decalogue also, then it never was binding because it was never ratified! (Some Sabbatarians say it was ratified by Christ at the

cross, Hebrews 9:15-17. Yet such is false and such would still mean it was not binding during the entire Old Testament period of history!).

2. This is indeed the ratification of the Decalogue, being then a part of the first covenant (Hebrews 9:18f, 1-4). Thus the Decalogue was not a binding covenant before its ratification at Sinai (Ibid. 9:17).

Exodus 31:13-16 — The sabbath, a sign between God and Israel (See 31:17f—One.2—Deuteronomy 5:15. Two.2).

Exodus 31:17f "It (sabbath) is a sign between me and the children of Israel forever: for in six days Jehovah made heaven and earth, and on the seventh day he rested, and was refreshed. And he gave unto Moses, when he had made an end of communing with him upon mount Sinai, the two tables of the testimony, tables of stone, written with the finger of God."

ASSERTIONS

One: The sabbath is to be kept forever.

Two: The ten commandments are the only laws written with the finger of God on stone, showing they cannot be erased.

ANSWERS

One: Concerning the word "forever"

1. The word "forever" here means throughout the generations of Israel (V 13,16,17). Thus the sabbath was to last as long as Israel (national) remained under the old covenant or "till" the faith should come (Galatians 3:19ff: cf Matthew 5:17).

2. The sabbath which was to last forever was a **perpetual covenant** only regarding Israel and not the Gentile nations (V. 16f). The sabbath was a "sign" showing

Israel was the only true nation of God (V. 13,17). Yet, if the rest of the nations kept the sabbath, as some did keep the rest of the moral laws (Romans 2:14), then it would not have been a sign at all. It would not have set Israel apart. Israel would have been like many other nations that did likewise. The truth is no other nation was charged with keeping the sabbath, did not keep the sabbath, and Israel's keeping it set her apart from the rest of the nations (See Deuteronomy 5:1-15 - Two.2). Note: Also, only Israel practiced the punishment prescribed in verses fourteen and fifteen (See Numbers 15:32-36).

3. Other covenants and conditions were mentioned to last "forever": circumcision (Genesis 17:13); Israel to possess Canaan forever (Ibid 13:15); the Passover to be observed forever (Exodus 12:14); the lamp to be kept burning in the tabernacle forever (Ibid. 27:21; cf 30:8); the day of atonement to last forever (Leviticus 16:29-31); etc. Even Sabbatarians admit that all of these ceased to be binding at the cross. Thus the word "forever" cannot be made to mean eternally when used concerning the sabbath.

Two: The ten commandments being written on stone with the finger of God has nothing to do with permanency as a covenant—never to be erased or cancelled.

1. First, such isn't literal. God has no literal, physical finger (Deuteronomy 4:15; Luke 24:39; John 4:24). Such is merely an anthropomorphism (application of human characteristics to deity - cf Exodus 33:23; Daniel 5:5). Thus the term is figurative and simply means the tablets were engraven by the power of God (See Exodus 8:19; Luke 11:20 - for the same expression).

2. Second, the tablets, supposedly indestructible because they were written on stone with God's finger, have long since been destroyed! Moses, a mere man, destroyed

the first set (Exodus 32:19), and the second set likely was destroyed by the time of the Babylonian captivity, 586 BC. (cf Josephus' Wars Bk V-Ch. 5-5). Thus the God-engraven-tablets of stone were not so permanent, physically speaking, after all. God originally recorded the basic tenants of his covenant (ten commandments) on stone to be a testimony to Israel and not in order that they might be preserved until the end of time (Genesis 28:18; 31:44-49). All the words of God, regardless of how or on what written, are in a sense indestructible (Isaiah 40:8). Yet such does not mean all the words of God shall be binding forever.

3. Third, those commandments written on stones were abolished at the cross (II Corinthians 3:6ff).

4. Fourth, the New Testament, given by the very person of God, Jesus Christ (Hebrews 1:2), and written on our hearts (Ibid. 8:10), is God's final word and authority which will last eternally (Matthew 28:18-20: Hebrews 13:20; I Peter 1:25).

Exodus 34:21-- Sabbath to be kept in all seasons.

Exodus 34:27f "And Jehovah said unto Moses, Write thou these words: for after the tenor of these words I have made a covenant with thee and with Israel...And he wrote upon the tables the words of the covenant, the ten commandments."

GOOD POINTS

One: The ten commandment covenant was with Israel (V. 27; See Deuteronomy 5:1-15; 29:1).

Two: Two covenants (one moral and one ceremonial) were not given to Israel at Sinai. This is quite obvious from this text and many others (Deuteronomy 4:13; 5:2; 29:1 - "**a, the** covenant").

Three: It is this ten commandment covenant which was done away at the cross (II Corinthians 3:6ff; Romans 7:1 9; Hebrews 8:6ff; 9:1-4; with 10:9).

Exodus 35:3 "Ye shall kindle no fire throughout your habitations upon the sabbath day."

GOOD POINTS

One: This shows the sabbath was not meant to be observed in all the world. Fire for warmth was not absolutely needed in Palestine. Thus this regulation more concerned itself with kindling a fire for cooking than for heating. Yet fire is needed for heating in colder climates (Alaska, etc.), showing this commandment was meant only for the Jews in Palestine and not for all men around the globe.

Two: Sabbatarians say all of the Old Testament is binding except that which was specifically abolished in the New Testament. Thus many of the sabbath regulations they still adhere to as kept under the Old Testament, for they were not specifically abolished in the New. Yet this **commandment** concerning the kindling of a fire was never specifically abolished! Thus why don't they keep it and punish those who kindle fires on the sabbath in heating and cooking? Strict Jews still do not cook food on the sabbath, and the Karaite Jews do not have fire or light in their houses even on very cold days on the sabbath. I reckon Sabbatarians know more about keeping sabbath than the Jews—those who received the Sinaitic covenant (Romans 3:2; 9:4)!

LEVITICUS

Leviticus 16:29-34 — The day of atonement. It was to be a day of **rest**, no work, and an **everlasting** statute (cf 23: 32).
Leviticus 19:3,30 — Israel commanded to keep all of God's sabbaths (See Exodus 20:8-11).

Leviticus 23:1-8 — The seventh-day sabbath was one of the set feasts which were abolished at the cross (Colossians 2:16; See Nunbers 28:9). It actually heads the list of such feasts!

Leviticus 23:11 – The feast of firstfruits was one day after the sabbath, Sunday (Numbers 28:26).

Good Point: Christ, having been raised from the dead on Sunday, is our firstfruits and has given us a new day to commemorate such, Sunday (I Corinthians 15:20; Psalms 118:22-24; Acts 20:7).

Leviticus 23:15-21 – The day of Pentecost or feast of weeks (Deuteronomy 16:9-12; See footnote 2).

Leviticus 23:24 – Israelites to rest on the day of blowing of trumpets.

Leviticus 23:32 – The day of atonement is a sabbath day (cf 16:29-34; See Genesis 2:2f - One 3).

Leviticus 23:37f "These are the set feasts of Jehovah, which ye shall proclaim to be holy convocations, to offer an offering made by fire unto Jehovah, a burnt offering, and a meal-offering, a sacrifice, and drink-offerings, each on its own day; besides the sabbaths of Jehovah, and besides your gifts, and besides all your vows, and besides all all your free-will-offerings, which ye give unto Jehovah."

ASSERTION: The ceremonial days and feasts are here kept separate—"besides"—from the sabbath. Thus the sabbath was not abolished with such ceremonial ordinances (Colossians 2:14-17).

ANSWER: Not only is the sabbath separate in this text, other so-called ceremonial ordinances are mentioned as separate: "**besides** offerings, gifts, vows." If this passage separates the sabbath as permanent (by using the word "besides"), then all the other ceremonial items are also separated as permanent. If not, why not? Actually, this was not so listed to exalt one day or activity above another but to separate the yearly observations (set feasts, each falling on one day—"its own day"—in the year) from the weekly (sabbaths, etc.).

Leviticus 23:39—The sabbath of the feast of the tabernacles (cf V. 34, 42f; Deuteronomy 16:13, 16).

Leviticus 24:8 — Provision of the lamp and bread in the sanctuary on the sabbath (cf I Chronicles 9:32; See Matthew 12:5 and Mark 2:23-28).

Leviticus 25:2-6 — The yearly sabbath (cf Exodus 23:10f).

Leviticus 25:8-12 — The Jubilee was, as far as tillage was concerned, a sabbatical year.

Leviticus 26:2 — Charge to Israel to keep the sabbaths.

Leviticus 26:34f, 43 — A sabbath of the land, during the chastisement, promised to Israel (See II Chronicles 36:21).

NUMBERS

Numbers 15:32-36 "And while the children of Israel were in the wilderness, they found a man gathering sticks upon the sabbath day. V.33 And they that found him gathering sticks brought him unto Moses and Aaron, and unto all the congregation. V.34 And they put him in ward, because it had not been declared what should be done unto him. V. 35 And Jehovah said unto Moses, The man shall surely be put to death: all the congregations shall stone him with stones without the camp. V.36 And all the congregation brought him without the camp, and stoned him to death with stones: as Jehovah commanded Moses."

GOOD POINTS:

One: This proves that the sabbath command, with its sundry regulations, was a new institution for the Israelites. They were not used to keeping it as such a stern command that the violation of it meant the death penalty (cf Exodus 31:14f; 35:2). Man had not, as Sabbatarians assert, been keeping the sabbath for 2500 years; he was in no way familiar with keeping it or its regulations!

Two: If one removes all the sundry regulations, such as this, from the keeping of the sabbath, then it would cease to be a sabbath day, a **rest** day. For one could work, play, and do anything morally good on that day. Thus the Sabbatarian, by allowing the abolishment of these "laws of Moses" has taken away the very basis for the keeping of the sabbath–the prohibition of working on it! Of course, the New Testament does not demand that one cease from working on the seventh day. Thus the Sabbatarian has nowhere to go (since he allowed the law of Moses to be abolished, and since the New Testament does not help him out on rest-regulations) to back up his contention that Christians ought to **rest** on the seventh day. If he goes to the Old Testament regulations to do such, then he not only must bring in the entire law of Moses as binding (Galatians 5:3), but he must also enforce the punishment for such sabbath violations. He does neither!

Numbers 23:20 — Sabbath blessing cannot be reversed??? (See Genesis 2:2f - Two-2).

Numbers 28:9 — The Jewish offerings on the sabbath.

GOOD POINT: The sabbath day is found right in the **middle** of the Jewish feasts and holy days, which days were abolished (See Colossians 2:16). Notice the list of holy days in order:

Daily ......(V.3-8)

Weekly . . .(V.9f) the sabbaths

Monthly . . . (V. 11-15)

Yearly . . . .(V. 16ff)

See similar lists in Leviticus 23:144; I Chronicles 23:30f; II Chronicles 2:4; 8:13; 31:3; Nehemiah 10:33; Isaiah 1:13f; Ezekiel 45:17; Hosea 2:11.

DEUTERONOMY

Deuteronomy 5:1-15 "And Moses called unto all Israel, and said unto them, Hear, O Israel, the statutes and the ordinances which I speak in your ears this day, that ye may learn them, and observe to do them. V.2 Jehovah our God made a covenant with us in Horeb. V.3 Jehovah made not this covenant with our fathers, but with us, even us, who are all of us here alive this day. V.4-14 - The giving of the Decalogue rehearsed. V.15 And thou shalt remember that thou wast a servant in the land of Egypt, and Jehovah thy God brought thee out thence by a mighty hand and by an outstretched arm; therefore Jehovah thy God commanded thee to keep the sabbath day."

ASSERTIONS

One: Just because God made the ten commandment covenant with the Jews at Sinai does not mean the ten commandments did not exist before Sinai (though not as such a formal covenant with one nation). For was it wrong to commit murder (sixth commandment) before Sinai? It most certainly was! Thus the breaking of the sabbath command would also be wrong before Sinai.

Two: The sabbath was to be kept by all men in remembrance of God's resting (Exodus 20:11) and not just by the nation of Israel in respect. of the Sinaitic covenant.

ANSWERS

One: Just because it was wrong to murder before the giving of the Sinaitic covenant does not mean it was wrong to fail to keep the sabbath. The Bible tells us mur- der was wrong before Sinai (Genesis 4:8ff; 9:6); but where before the Exodus account, does the Bible say it was wrong to not rest on the seventh day? It doesn't! It was not wrong to not keep the rest of the seventh day until God made it wrong, sanctified it as the sabbath day. And, since God never commanded the Gentiles to keep it, then it was never wrong for them to not keep it, especially since it was not an inherently moral principle (See Exodus 20:8-11 - Two. 2; Genesis 2:2f - Four. 2).

Two: The sabbath was not kept even by Israel just to remember God's resting, much less by all nations of men. There are two other reasons why Israel alone kept the sabbath:

1. Israel kept the sabbath because God commanded them to keep it (Exodus 16:23-30) and not just because they wanted to commemorate God's resting at the creation. Now God included this sabbath command in the covenant he made at Sinai (Exodus 20:8-11), in the ten commandment covenant (Deuteronomy 4:13; 5:1-15). Thus the authority for anyone keeping the sabbath is this covenant; no one would even know to keep it apart from it. Yet God only made this covenant with the nation of Israel (Deuteronomy 4:8; 5:1; cf Psalms 147:20; Amos 3:2; Romans 3:2; 9:4). Thus the Gentiles were never asked nor obligated to keep it. Even the Jewish fathers (Abraham, Isaac and Jacob) who lived before the Sinaitic covenant were not bound to keep it or any such covenant (Deuteronomy 5:3; 1:8; cf 11:2-7. (Moses was the

mediator of this covenant and the first Jewish Father to keep the sabbath—John 1:17; 7:19; Galatians 3:17-19.)

2. Israel, as this text clearly states (V.15), was to keep the sabbath as a "sign" of their deliverance from Egyptian bondage and not as a "memorial" of God's creation-rest (cf Exodus 31:17f - One.2). Now it is true that God chose the seventh day to be the day of rest because it had been a day of rest for him; yet he gave it to them to remember their rest from the serfdom of Egypt and not his rest (Deuteronomy 5:15; cf Exodus 1:11-14). Thus the sabbath was not kept before this deliverance, the Exodus, and it was not kept by any other nation, for only Israel was so delivered. This agrees with all the other accounts as to the giving of the sabbath and ten commandments after Egyptian bondage and not before (I Kings 8:9,21; Nehemiah 9:13f; Ezekiel 20:10-12; Malachi 4:4; Hebrews 8:9; cf II Corinthians 3:6ff). Therefore, **all men** were not obligated to keep the sabbath for any reason, either because of the authority of the ten commandment covenant (for it was given only to Israel at Sinai) or in commemoration of God's resting at the creation (for even the Jews, much less the Gentiles, are not recorded as keeping it for that reason).

Note: The sabbath was the weekly reminder of Israel's deliverance from Egyptian bondage, and the Passover was the yearly reminder. Both of these were instituted after Egypt and for the Jews only (cf Exodus 12:14ff). Christians have a new **sign** on a new **day** to commemorate a far greater, antitypical (I Corinthians 10:1f) **deliverance:** the Lord's Supper, partaken on the first day of the week (Acts 20:7) commemorates (I Corinthians 11:24) our deliverance from the bondage of the law and sin (I Corinthians 15:56f; Galatians 5:1; Colossians 2:14ff).

Deuteronomy 5:22 "These words Jehovah spake unto all your assembly in the mount out of the midst of the fire, of the cloud, and of the thick darkness, with a great voice: and he added no more. And he wrote them upon two tables of stone, and gave them unto me."

ASSERTION: God added no more to the ten commandment covenant than that which was on the two tablets of stone (Cf Exodus 34:28).

ANSWER: This has nothing to do with what was contained in the Sinaitic covenant, which had as its basis the ten commandments. Nowhere in this text does it say that God added no more to the covenant than the ten commandments. Such can only be read into the text and not out of it! This simply states that God spoke only that which was contained on the two tablets unto the entire assembly. The rest of the covenant, including the other laws, statutes and ordinances, was mediated through Moses and not spoken directly to the people. All the words of God spoken at Sinai, whether directly or mediately, were still his words and equally authoritative (II Timothy 3:16; II Peter 1:21; Jeremiah 1:7, 9; See Deuteronomy 31: 24-26 for a refutation of exalting the Decalogue over the law of Moses).

Deuteronomy 9:10—See Exodus 31:17f—Two.

Deuteronomy 10:5 — The ten commandments were placed inside the ark to show (supposedly) how they were to be a separate covenant from the Mosaical law (See 31:24-26).

Deuteronomy 31:24-26 "And it came to pass, when Moses had made an end of writing the words of this law in a book, until they were finished, that Moses commanded the Levites, that bare the ark of the covenant of Jehovah, saying, Take this book of the law, and put it by the side of the ark of the covenant of Jehovah your God, that it may be there for a witness against thee."

ASSERTIONS

One: The ten commandments, written by God himself, were placed **inside** the ark (Deuteronomy 10:5). They are thus God's most holy laws, his separate and eternal covenant (Revelation 11:19).

Two: The book of Moses, or ceremonial covenant, was placed **outside**—"by the side"—of the ark and not in it. This shows the law of Moses was not equal to the law of God or the Lord, the ten commandment law. It was the only one abolished at the cross.

ANSWERS

One: The placing of the ten commandments **inside** the ark was not for the purpose of exalting them above the laws mediated through Moses nor to distinguish them as a separate and eternal covenant.

1. Where is such a theory to be read in this text? There's not even enough room between the lines in this short text to read in such a complicated theory!

2. The placing of the ten commandments in the ark was for ceremonial reasons and no such conjectured reasons as asserted. The Decalogue, as all the old law (for which the Decalogue stood as representative of the whole, being the basic principles), pointed out the sins of the people which needed atoning for (Romans 3:20; 7:7). The mercy seat, situated on top of the ark over the tablets of stone, was to have the blood of atonement sprinkled on it, depicting God's forgiveness of their sins against the covenant in the ark (Exodus 25:21f;

Leviticus 16:2, 13ff). Indeed the law written on stones was rightly called the ministration of death (II Corinthians 3:7).

3. The placing of the ten commandments in the ark did not make it a separate and eternal covenant. (a) We have already seen how this entire covenant was only given to Israel to last throughout their generations (Exodus 31:17f). (b) Also, Aaron's budding rod and the pot of manna were in the ark (Exodus 16:33f; Numbers 17: 10; Hebrews 9:4). Were they to last eternally? Did their being in the ark make them more holy than the ceremonial ordinances contained in the book of Moses (outside the ark) which even brought about atonement for sins? (c) The ark and all the physical things in it— the tablets of stone, rod, and manna—have long since perished from the face of the earth. None lasted eternally. This shows they were only meant to be temporal—like the covenant with which they were related! (d) The very thought of the ark, as well as the other Old Testament types and shadows, has been removed by the establishment of Christ's New Testament (Jeremiah 3:16; Hebrews 8-10).

4. That placed inside the ark, the tables of stone, is called the old covenant of Moses, which covenant was abolished (II Corinthians 3:6f, 14f).

5. That covenant placed inside the ark is called the first covenant. This first covenant contained "ordinances" as well as moral laws (Hebrews 9:1-4). This first covenant was taken away when the second covenant was established (Ibid. 10:9).

6. That covenant placed inside the ark is unlike the new covenant: the tablets of stone in the ark were connected with the covenant God made with Israel **when** they came out of Egypt (I Kings 8:9; cf Deuteronomy 5:1-3, 15); the new covenant is **unlike** the cove-

nant God made with Israel when they came out of Egypt (Hebrews 8:9). Thus the Decalogue is not the new covenant—the two are unalike!

7. Revelation 11:19 has nothing to do with Christians keeping the law contained in the ark (seen in heaven) on the earth (See Revelation 11:19 for discussion).

Two: The book of Moses placed **by the side** (outside) of the ark was not a separate and inferior covenant from the Decalogue inside the ark.

1. **This "book of the law" (the law of Moses only, according to Sabbatarians) placed outside the ark contained all the words of the Lord (Exodus 24:4; 34:27).** Now the ten commandments made up part of the words that Moses wrote in this book. (The Hebrew for ten commandments is "ten words "). They are still in the book of Moses. Read Exodus 20:3-17 and Deuteronomy 5:7-21 and see! Thus that which was outside the ark (so-called ceremonial law) contained the words of that which was inside the ark (moral laws). If the contents of the book outside the ark were abolished, then so were the words of the ten commandments which were in that book (cf Romans 7:1-7)!

2. The "book of the law" refers to the first five books of Moses in their entirety, the Pentateuch (Galatians 3: 10).

The book of Genesis (3:16) . . . . . . See I Corinthians 14:34
The book of Exodus (20:17) . . . . . See Romans 7:7.
(20:25) . . . . . . See Joshua 8:31.
The book of Leviticus (19:18) . . . . See Matthew 22:36-40
The book of Numbers (28:9f) . . . . See Matthew 12:5.
The book of Deuteronomy (6:5) . . See Matthew 22:36-40.
(24:16) . . . . .See II Kings 14:6.

3. This "book of the law" included the ten commandments.

The fifth command....See Mark 7:10.

The sixth command... See John 7:19.

Note: The penalty for breaking the law of Moses was the same as for violations of the ten commandments (Hebrews 10:28; Galatians 3:10f; Exodus 31:14; Deuteronomy 17:6).

4. This "book of the law" contained laws greater than all the laws of the Decalogue put together (Mark 12:30f; Matthew 22:36-40). These two greatest of laws, on which all law hangs (even the Decalogue), are found outside the Decalogue—thus outside the ark also and in the so-called ceremonial law of Moses (Leviticus 19:18: Deuteronomy 6:5). If these two greatestof laws were abolished when the "law of Moses" was abolished, then so also fell the Decalogue which hung upon them! Of course, these two laws are everlasting principles, and they are repeatedly exemplified and alluded to throughout the New Testament. Thus, though abolished with the entire old law system, they are carried on in the new(Romans 13:8-10).

5. This "book of the law" (law of Moses) is often called the "law of God" (Joshua 24:26: I Kings 2:3: II Chronicles 33:8; 34:14; Ezra 7:6,12: Nehemiah 8:1-3.7f, 14:18; 10:29). Thus the Sabbatarian's distinction between the law of God (supposedly only the Decalogue) and the law of Moses does not exist in the Bible. In fact, the terms "the law, law of God" are never found referring to the entire Decalogue alone. Such a notion is unscriptural, nonscriptural and antiscriptural. See Galatians 3:19 where even they say the term "the law" is referring to the ceremonial law and not the moral!

6. The law of Moses is also called the "law of the Lord" (again supposedly just the Decalogue is so called Leviticus 12:8 and II Chronicles 31:4 with Luke 2:22-27).

The law of the Lord contained more than just moral commandments (the ten commandments); it also contained ceremonial rites and sabbaths (II Chronicles 31:3). Now, if the law of the Lord was not abolished at the cross, then neither were these ceremonial rites and sabbaths (as Sabbatarians say Colossians 2:16 refers to)!

7. The law of Moses contained many moral laws (Sabbatarians say just ceremonial), including murder and adultery (Deuteronomy 27:15-26; See Ephesians 2:15).

Thus the so-called two covenants (the law of God, being the moral laws of the Decalogue inside the ark; the law of Moses, being the ceremonial laws written in the book and placed outside the ark) do not exist as such. Where in all of the Bible does it say there was a separate "ceremonial covenant" (book of the law) distinct from a "moral covenant" (Decalogue)? Find even the words "ceremonial and moral covenants" in the Bible. Why doesn't any New Testament writer ever say that only the ceremonial book of the law was abolished and the moral law of the Decalogue was established (Romans 3:31 - no distinction mentioned)?

Only one covenant issued forth from Sinai, and it contained **all the words of God**— the ten commandments (inside the ark) and all written by Moses in the book of the law, including a written record of the ten commandments (Deuteronomy 29:1; Galatians 4:21-31). It contained moral, ceremonial and civil laws, but it was only one covenant. By way of illustration, Christ, though being one person, was called a **lion** and a **lamb** (Revelation 5:5f).

Note: The civil government is no longer ruled by specific laws in God's new covenant (as was Israel under the Old Testament). The reason for this is that God's new kingdom is a spiritual kingdom and not a national one (John 18:36). Now such political governing and law-making has been relegated to the civil governments of the world (Romans 13:1ff).

JOSHUA
N/A
JUDGES
N/A
RUTH
N/A
FIRST SAMUEL
N/A
SECOND SAMUEL
N/A

FIRST KINGS

I Kings 8:9—Only the two tables of stone remained in the ark at this point in time (See Deuteronomy 31:24-26 One 5; cf Hebrews 8:9).

SECOND KINGS

II Kings 4:23—The sabbath was one of the days when the pious people of Israel sought instruction from the prophets' mouths in their houses (cf Keil and Delitzsch).

II Kings 11:5,7,9—Division and distribution of the royal guard on the sabbath to protect king Joash.

II Kings 16:18—The covered place in the court of the temple for the king and his party when visits were made on the sabbath and feast days (cf Keil and Delitzsch).

II Kings 21:8—The Sabbatarian assertion that this text teaches two separate laws were given in the Old Testament —God's "I have commanded" and Moses' "Moses commanded"— is utterly false and completely refuted in Deuteronomy 31:24-26. Also, this very text is quoted in II Chronicles 33:8, and it says **all** the commandments were given **by** God **through** Moses!

FIRST CHRONICLES

I Chronicles 9:32—Preparation of the showbread on the Sabbath by the priests (cf Leviticus 24:5-8; See Matthew 12:5; Mark 2:23-28).

I Chronicles 16:15-18 "Remember his covenant forever, The word which he commanded to a thousand generations, The covenant which he made with Abraham, And his oath unto Isaac, and confirmed the same unto Jacob for a statute, To Israel for an everlasting covenant, Saying, Unto thee will I give the land of Canaan, The lot of your inheritance."

ASSERTION: The ten commandment covenant was to last a thousand generations. Not even a third of such has yet been completed. Thus it still is binding as a covenant.

ANSWER: The ten commandments are not mentioned as the covenant under consideration in this text, and the thousand generations cannot be literal.

1. The covenant mentioned in this text is not the Decalogue or the Law of Moses; it is that covenant (or unconditional promise) made with Abraham and the rest of the fathers hundreds of years before any such codified law system was given (V.16f; Galatians 3:15-17). It was God's covenant promise to give the land of Canaan unto Israel (Abraham's seed) and not heaven to those who would keep the ten commandments (V.18; cf Genesis 15:18; 26:3; 28:13).

2. The term "thousand generations" is not literal. The number, one-thousand, usually stresses ultimate completeness in the Bible; just as the words "forever, everlasting" mean the entire time period ordained by God for something to exist or be in force(cf Deuteronomy 1:11; 5:10; 7:9; Psalms 50:10; 84:10; 90:4; 105:8; II Peter 3:8). Psalms 50:10 says all the cattle on a thousand

hills are God's. Now, if this is taken literally, then to whom belongs the cattle on hill number 1001? Thus our text under discussion simply refers to all the generations of Israel and no one else (V.13; See Exodus 31:17f—One.1). Also, if taken literally as Sabbatarians are wont to do, then the ten commandment covenant would still be abolished one day—at the end of the thousand generations. Then what will become of their theory that the sabbath (a part of the ten commandment covenant) will be kept forever, even throughout all eternity? A thousand generations is not eternity!

I Chronicles 17:27—The sabbath blessed forever??? (See Genesis 2:2f—Two.3).

I Chronicles 23:30f—Sundry holy days, sabbaths and feasts (See Numbers 28:9; cf Colossians 2:16).

SECOND CHRONICLES

II Chronicles 2:4; 8:13; 31:3—Lists of the holy days (See Numbers 28:9; cf Colossians 2:16).

II Chronicles 23:4,8—See II Kings 11:5,7,9.

II Chronicles 36:21—Sabbath of the land of Israel during captivity (cf Leviticus 26:34f,43; Lamentations 2:6).

EZRA
N/A

NEHEMIAH

Nehemiah 9:14 "And (God) madest known unto them thy holy sabbath, and commandedst them commandments (the moral law or the Decalogue), and statutes, and a law, by Moses thy servant (ceremonial law)."

ASSERTION: This shows one law, the ten commandment

law, was given directly by God and another law, containing statutes (ceremonial), was given by Moses.

ANSWER: It is true that God gave different parts of the Old Testament law in different manners (Hebrews 1:1); but such does not mean every part given differently constituted a different law.

1. Only one law is under consideration in this text, God's law as given through Moses (Nehemiah 8:1-3, 7f,14,18; 10:29). Even the Decalogue was given to Israel through the hands of Moses, inasmuch as he brought the tablets down from the mount (See Deuteronomy 31:24-26-Two.3).

2. This text says the law containing the sabbath was given at Sinai (V.13), refuting the Sabbatarian's contention that it was given to Adam (See Deuteronomy 5:1-15; See Deuteronomy 31:24-26 for a thorough refutation of the so-called "two law" theory).

Nehemiah 10:31—Prohibition of trading on the sabbath (cf 13:15-22; Amos 8:5-9).

Nehemiah 10:33—A list of the holy days (See Numbers 28:9; cf Colossians 2:16).

Nehemiah 13:15-22—Violations of the sabbath in Israel. Notice the gates of the city were to be closed on the sabbath day (V.19; cf Jeremiah 17:27; See Matthew 24:20).

ESTHER
N/A

JOB

GOOD POINT: The book of Job is reputed by many scholars to be the most ancient book recorded in the Bible. Yet the sabbath is nowhere mentioned in it. Surely, such a righteous man as Job would have said that he kept the sabbath if it was always kept by the righteous, such as Adam, Abel, Enoch, etc. (Job 1:1,8)!

PSALMS

Psalms 19:7 "The law of Jehovah is perfect, restoring the soul."

ASSERTIONS

One: The ten commandment law is God's perfect law which cannot be changed.

Two: The ceremonial law was entirely unlike the Decalogue and could make nothing perfect (cf Hebrews 7:19). Thus it was the imperfect law which was abolished at the cross.

ANSWERS

One: There is absolutely no reason in this context to limit this law to the Decalogue.

1. The term "the law" refers—nine out of ten times—to the entire Pentateuch and not just to the Decalogue (if it ever refers to it as a whole alone). The term "the law of Jehovah" is also used in reference to the Mosaical law and not just the Decalogue (See Deuteronomy 31:24-26—Two 5-6). Also, David, the writer of this chapter, was a king of Israel and was thus required to keep a copy of the entire law of Moses and not just the Decalogue(Deuteronomy 17:15-20; cf Psalms 119:128 . Therefore, according to the Sabbatarian's assertion, the entire law of Moses could not be changed, for it was also perfect!

2. Just because a law is perfect (complete for the purpose for which it was designed) does not mean it cannot be changed. The entire old law (Decalogue included) was perfect only for the purpose for which it was designed—to be a tutor to drive men to Christ and his law of faith (Galatians 3:19-26). It was not perfect as a system of salvation. If it would have been, then there would have been no need for Christ's becoming our Saviour (Galatians 2:21; 3:21f).

Two: The so-called ceremonial law of Moses was as perfect as the Decalogue.

1. This text says so. We have seen that the term "the law of Jehovah" cannot be limited to the Decalogue alone. Thus the entire Old Testament law was perfect.

2. The law of Moses was also given by God (Ezra 7:6; See Deuteronomy 31:24-26-Two. 5). Now, since none of God's works are imperfect, then the law of Moses, a work of God, was perfect (cf Deuteronomy 32:4; II Samuel 22:31). Also, I would like to ask the Sabbatarian to point out any imperfections in the law of Moses as far as a legal law system is concerned. One cannot improve upon the Old Testament law system as a civil and moral code. Unless one would abolish legal law as the only motivation unto purity and faithfulness and replace it with a law of liberty and love. Thus the law of Moses was perfect for the purpose for which it was designed—to drive men to Christ and his law of liberty.

3. Hebrews 7:19 does not say the law of Moses is all that is under discussion. Such is only assumed by Sabbatarians (See Hebrews 7:19).

Psalms 40:7 "Then said I, Lo, I am come; In the roll of the book it is written of me: I delight to do thy will, O my God; Yes, thy law is within my heart" (cf Hebrews 10:7).

ASSERTION: This is a prophecy telling how Jesus would keep the ten commandment law. Thus so must we.

ANSWER: This does not say the "ten commandment law" was all that was in his heart. It says "thy law," and such means all of God's law.

1. David is speaking typically here (Jesus being the antitype - Hebrews 10:7), and he no doubt has in mind the book of the law (often contained in rolls) which

he was to possess and lay to heart (See Deuteronomy 17:15-20; Psalms 19:7 - One.1). Notice David refers to the "roll of the book" and not to the "tablets of the Decalogue!"

2. Jesus delighted to keep all the laws of Moses and not just the ten commandments (See Mark 1:21; cf Galatians 4:4). Why don't Sabbatarians do likewise?

3. Jesus fulfilled the entire Old Testament by so keeping it (Matthew 5:17f); and then he abolished it (Ephesians 2:15; Colossians 2:14-17).

Psalms 89:28-36 "My lovingkindness will I keep for him for evermore; And my covenant shall stand fast with him... V.34 My covenant will I. not break, Nor alter the thing that is gone out of my lips."

ASSERTION: God here promised that he would never change his ten commandment covenant.

ANSWER: The covenant under discussion in this text has nothing at all to do with either the Decalogue or the law of Moses. It is God's covenant with David that He would set one of his seed (Christ) on his throne forever (V.3f,27,35f; cf II Samuel 7:12-16; Acts 2:29-36). Notice also that mention is made of laws in this text other than the ten commandments, e.g., "ordinances" **(V.30) and** "statutes" (V.31). Were they also never changed or abolished? Why, even Sabbatarians admit they were!

Psalms 92 (Title)—"A song for the sabbath day"

Psalms 95:11—Israel was prohibited from entering God's true rest (cf Deuteronomy 12:9; See **Hebrews 4:1-11).**

Psalms 111:7f —"The works of his hands are truth and

justice; All his precepts (commandments-KJV) are sure. They are established for ever and ever..."

ASSERTION: God's ten commandments will remain established forever.

ANSWER: There is no mention of the ten commandments in this text. Such is only assumed. This says "all of his commandments" and not just a select few! Thus anything God commanded applies. The Hebrew word used for "commandments" also refers to precepts and statutes (See Exodus 31:17f—One, on the word "forever").

Psalms 118:22-24 — The day the Lord made - "The Lord's Day" (See Revelation 1:10).

Psalms 119 (Read the entire chapter)

ASSERTION: Every verse in this chapter indicates that God's ten commandment laws are holy and to last forever (cf V.1,44).

ANSWER: Again and again Sabbatarians make the same unwarranted assumption (unscriptural addition - Revelation 22:18), that the words "ten commandments" are in the text when they are not. The entire Old Testament law is under consideration in this chapter and not just the ten commandment laws. Neither can it be restricted to laws or commandments, for more is under discussion than such. "Statutes" are included (V.5,8,23,26,33,48,54,64,68,71,80,83, 112,117,118,124,135,145,155). "Ordinances" are also included (V.13,20,30,39,43,52,62,91,102,106,108,149,156,160,164,175). (Notice V.160 says the "ordinances" were to last "forever"! See Exodus 31:17f on the word "forever".) Thus, according to the Sabbatarian's assertion, all the Old Testament statutes and ordinances were to last forever. Even they deny such.

PROVERBS

Proverbs 28:9 "He that turneth his ear away from hearing the law, Even his prayer is an abomination."

ASSERTION: Only those who keep the ten commandment law (fourth command included) are heard in prayer.

ANSWER: Again the words "ten commandment" are not present. And, since the law under discussion contained all the ceremonial precepts as well as the Decalogue, then the Sabbatarians are not heard in prayer either, for they do not keep them all (cf Deuteronomy 31:24-26)!

ECCLESIASTES

Ecclesiastes 12:13 "This is the end of the matter; all hath been heard: fear God, and keep his commandments; for this is the whole duty of man."

ASSERTIONS

One: The keeping of the ten commandments is the whole duty of man.

Two: The ceremonial duties (of Mosaical law) of man were temporal and abolished at the cross (Hebrews 9:9f).

ANSWERS

One: This text does not say keeping the ten commandments was man's only duty.

1. The word "ten" is not in the text. It is assumed as usual. The whole of God's law was under consideration when Solomon, who lived in the most glorious age of the Mosaical law, wrote this. Which part of the Old Testament law could he or his subjects ignore as their duty to keep? If they were not bound to keep all the ceremonial requirements of the law, then why did

Solomon expend so much time, money and effort to have a great temple constructed in which the priests could carry out the ceremonial duties?

2. Where in the Bible does it say man's whole duty (thus his only duty) is just to keep the ten commandments? It doesn't even say such a thing in the Old Testament, even to those who lived under the ten commandment covenant! It was also their divinely determined duty to be circumcised (Genesis 17:10-14). It is now our duty to be baptized (Mark 16:16; Acts 10:48—commanded). Yet there is no way either one of these duties can be found demanded, inferred or hinted at in the ten commandments. It is man's duty to do anything God asks him to do—either to build an ark, offer up his only son, or to be baptized. It is just as much his duty to do any of these things as it is to obey the command not to murder!

Two: Their appealing to Hebrews 9:9f for man's ceremonial duties (abolished at the cross) is entirely without force, for this text only deals with the Old Testament priests' service in the temple and not some so-called ceremonial duties of all men. I might add that Hebrews, chapter nine, also includes a few words about the ten commandments as being the first covenant, containing ordinances (so-called ceremonial duties), which was done away (Hebrews 9:1-4; 10:9)!

SONG OF SOLOMON

N/A

ISAIAH

Isaiah 1:13 —Formalistic sabbath keeping of the Jews condemned (cf Amos 8:5). Also, here is another list of the holy days (See Numbers 28:9; Colossians 2:16).

Isaiah 2:3 — God's new law (covenant) to go forth from

Jerusalem and not Sinai, meaning from the physical city of Jerusalem (Luke 24:47; Acts 1:8) as well as the spiritual Jerusalem, the church (Galatians 4:21-31; Hebrews 12:18-24; cf Micah 4:2).

Isaiah 42:21 "It pleased Jehovah, for his righteousness' sake, to magnify his law, and make it honorable."

ASSERTIONS

One: This is prophetic of how the Messiah would magnify and honor the ten commandment law.

Two: If Christ abolished the ten commandment law, he dishonored it.

ANSWERS

One: This text does not refer to, nor make mention of, Christ or the ten commandment law.

1. The context (V. 18-25) does not demand that the "servant" of verse nineteen (to which verse twenty-one relates) be the same as the "servant" of verse one (which is definitely the Messiah). Rather, this context favors Israel as being the servant (cf 41:8). God had given his law to Israel at Sinai for the purpose of making them a great and holy nation—thus bringing honor to, or magnifying, his laws through their righteous example (V.21; cf Exodus 19:6). Yet, had they honored his law? NO! They rather chose to be blind to all of God's workings and deaf to all of his laws (V.18f, 23f; 43:8). (This shows this servant could not be the Messiah, for he certainly wasn't blind and deaf as mentioned in this context!) Thus they, by their faithlessness and present inglorious condition (V.22), had brought reproach rather than honor upon God's law. Therefore, this text actually has nothing to do with what the Messiah would do to the law (any law) when he would come (See Pulpit Commentary; Keil & Delitzsch).

2. Also, as usual, there is no mention of the "ten commandment law" in this verse (V.21). The "law" here would include the entire Pentateuch and not just the Decalogue. Thus, according to the Sabbatarian's application of this text to the Messiah, all the Mosaical law was to be magnified as God's abiding law. This is false, and even they deny that all the Mosaical law is to be kept.

3. Christ did, in fact, magnify and honor all the Old Testament law (not just the Decalogue) in his earthly life and ministry. This he did by restoring it in its purity (pointing out the man-made traditions), keeping it perfectly, fulfilling all of its requirements and types and fully accomplishing its purpose (Galatians 3:19-26; See Romans 3:31). He then abolished it.

Two: Christ did not dishonor the ten commandment law in abolishing it as a legal covenant. To abolish something does not mean to dishonor it. Christ abolished the so-called ceremonial law of Moses (even according to Sabbaratians). Yet did his abolishing it dishonor it? No! Also, did his doing away with the Passover dishonor it? No! ETC.

Isaiah 56:4-6 "...V.6 Also The Foreigners that join themselves to Jehovah, to minister unto him, and to love the name of Jehovah, to be his servants, everyone that keepeth the sabbath from profaning it, and holdeth fast my covenant."

ASSERTION: This represents a clear prophecy of how the Gentiles—"foreigners"—would keep the sabbath in the Messianic or Christian Age.

ANSWER: This text makes no mention of Gentile "Christians" keeping sabbath in the "Messianic Age."

1. First of all, this context cannot be confined to only

a Messianic fulfillment. Its first and primary fulfillment resides with the return of the Jews from captivity. This particular context concerns itself with God's treatment of the "foreigners" who had become a part of Israel while Israel was amongst them. These foreigners (V.3,6- the heathen with Israel in the land of captivity), who had joined themselves to Jehovah and Israel, i.e., became proselytes (V.3,4,6; cf Exodus 12:48; Esther 8:17), were fearful that they would be cut off from Israel when Israel was delivered from captivity and brought back into their holy land (V. 5). So God here promised that those foreigners who loved him and kept his laws and covenants (all the Old Testament) would not be cut off in Palestine. They would worship with the chosen people in the holy mountain and temple (V.6f; cf I Kings 8:41-43). Thus this has nothing, as far as the primary fulfillment is concerned, to do with what Gentiles would do upon becoming Christians in the Messianic Age. Also, Christians are not obligated to do what Gentiles, who had become Jewish converts (as in this text), did long before the new covenant existed!

2. On the other hand, this text, no doubt, can be considered Messianic and typical of how God would treat the Gentiles in the coming Messianic kingdom. The Gentiles ("others"—V.8) would be gathered with the Jews and become one fold (John 10:16), worshipping together in spiritual Zion and the spiritual house of prayer, the universal church of Christ (Ephesians 2:11-15; I Peter 2:9f). Yet the terms used in this context cannot be pressed literally from their primary application (describing Gentile blessedness in Palestine after the Jews were delivered from captivity)into the secondary or antitypical application (their blessedness in the church). (a) First, the prophets commonly spoke such two-fold prophecies in plain Jewish terminology, applying such to those of their time and to the age to come (cf II Samuel

7:12ff). This is quite understandable and to be expected.

We also do the same thing. For example, a man living in the "horse and buggy days," before the automobile was invented, would naturally promise his young son a horse and buggy and not a car for his 21st birthday. Yet, if the automobile came into being before his birthday, then the giving of a car to him would not violate the promise. Thus the prophets, prophesying before the blessings of the Christian Age, used familiar blessings to relate future blessedness. One would certainly not have related future blessedness to the Jews by telling them their entire national heritage and religion, which they knew and loved, would be done away or superseded! Notice other Messianic prophecies using such Jewish terminology: David was foretold to be their king and shepherd, and God's tabernacle to be in their midst (Ezekiel 34:23ff; 37:24ff; cf John 10:11; Acts 2:29ff; Ephesians 2:21f); the tabernacle of David to be rebuilt (Amos 9:11; cf Acts 15:15ff; etc.).

Therefore, these Jewish terms are not (and were not by the Apostles) to be pressed literally into the Messianic Age. They were typical and were meant to be understood as symbolic of the spiritual blessedness in Messiah's spiritual kingdom. (b) Second, if these terms are pressed literally (as Sabbatarians say this means the Gentiles would keep the literal sabbath), then, according to verse seven of this same chapter, we should also have a literal "holy mountain" (contrary to John 4:20-24; Hebrews 12:18-23), a literal temple "house of prayer" (Matthew 21:12f; contrary to I Peter 2:5), and should offer up literal "burnt offerings and sacrifices" upon a literal "altar" (contrary to the spiritual things of I Peter 2:5; cf Hebrews 13:10). Even Sabbatarians reject such literal sacrifices. Yet, if one point, the sabbath, is to be literally understood, then all must be so understood. If not, why not? By the way, we have a far greater, antitypical sabbath-rest than did the Jews or do the Sabbatarians (Matthew 11:28; cf Hebrews 4:1-11; See Keil & Delitzsch and the Pulpit Commentary on this text in Isaiah).

Isaiah 58:13 "If thou turn away thy foot from the sabbath, from doing thy pleasure on my holy day; and call the sabbath a delight, and the holy of Jehovah honorable; and shalt honor it, not doing thine own ways, nor finding thine own pleasure, nor speaking thine own words: then shalt thou delight thyself in Jehovah. . . ."

ASSERTION: All those who are faithful and blessed keep the sabbath correctly.

ANSWER: This text does not apply in the least to what people in the Christian Age must do. It only applies to the Israelites of that particular Old Testament period: to the "house of Jacob" which was sinning (V.1,14 - in violating the sabbath - cf Jeremiah 17:21-23; Nehemiah 10:31; 13:15f): the people of Israel "as a nation" were being addressed (V.2); and repentance would bring restoration—"to rebuild the old waste places, foundations, walls" (V. 12). Thus this is speaking of the calling of the Jewish nation to repentance and not pointing out what faithful Christians must do!

Isaiah 66:22f "For as the new heavens and the new earth, which I will make, shall remain before me, saith Jehovah, so shall your seed and your name remain. And it shall come to pass, that from one new moon to another, and from one sabbath to another, shall all flesh come to worship before me, saith Jehovah."

ASSERTION: True worshippers shall keep the sabbath even in heaven— in the "new heavens and earth" (cf Revelation

21:1; See Revelation 11:19).

ANSWER: This does not teach the keeping of the sabbath in heaven, and their assertion is erroneous for many reasons:

1.Such is a total misunderstanding of the term "new heavens and earth." This term is also used in a two-fold manner by Isaiah, referring to the restoration of Judaism after Babylonian captivity (Isaiah 65:17ff) and the New Jerusalem, the church (Ibid. 66:22f; Revelation 21:1f,9f with Galatians 4:26ff; Hebrews 12:22f; See this writer's book "Second Peter Three-Jewish Calamity or Universal Climax?"). It thus, in both cases, finds fulfillment in time and not in eternity (cf Luke 24:44ff; Acts 3:18ff).

2.Such is to press literal meanings upon the Jewish terms used by the prophet in depicting the glories of the coming kingdom, the church (See Isaiah 56:4-6#2). By doing such, Sabbatarians find themself in a dilemma, for this text also says they will keep the "new moons from one to another." Even they say the keeping of new moons was abolished at the cross (Colossians 2:16). Thus they cannot use this text as a prophecy of what the church would do in time, much less eternity!

3. It will be impossible to keep the sabbath in heaven. There will be no days and nights there, just an "eternal day" (II Peter 3:18 margin). Thus there will be no such time periods to regulate our activities, no seventh days!

4.Heaven will be one eternal sabbath rest and not six days of work and one off (See Hebrews 4:1-11; cf Revelation 14:13). **Note:** The millenarian position that the "new heavens and earth" refers to a thousand year reign on earth or some earthly type heaven is utterly false (John 14:1-3; I Corinthians 15:24; I Thessalonians 4:13-18).

JEREMIAH

Jeremiah 3:16f "And it shall come to pass, when ye are multiplied and increased in the land, in those days, saith Jehovah, they shall say no more, The ark of the covenant of Jehovah; neither shall it come to mind; neither shall they remember it; neither shall they miss it; neither shall it be made any more. At that time they shall call Jerusalem the throne of Jehovah..."

GOOD POINT: The ark of the covenant is no longer central or important in the Christian Age ("multiplied and increased in the land" points to the Messianic Age - Jeremiah 23:3ff; Hosea 1:10f). From Sinai onward God's presence, authority (covenant with national Israel) and throne (footstool) were understood in the ark (Exodus 25:21f; Psalms 99:5; 132:7f). One could not and cannot think of the ark and not be reminded of the covenant (as the two tablets of stone inside it represented the entire covenant); nor can one continuously be reminded of the ten commandments, the two tablets, and not be reminded of the ark of the covenant. Thus both the ark and the covenant inside, the ten commandments, belong to old Israel and past memories. Yet now spiritual Jerusalem, the church (Galatians 4:21-31; Hebrews 12:22f), is understood as God's dwelling place and throne (heavenly), and his new law and covenant issues forth from it and not Sinai (See Isaiah 2:2f; cf Hebrews 9:1-4; 10:9; Deuteronomy 31:24-26).

Jeremiah 17:21-27-God's charge to the Jews to hallow the sabbath or Jerusalem would be destroyed. See Nehemiah 13:17f where they were reminded, after Jerusalem had been destroyed, of this fulfillment (cf Lamentations 2:6).

Jeremiah 31:31-34-God promised to make a new covenant which would be entirely **unlike** the old Sinaitic covenant.

The very mention of a **new** covenant indicated the present covenant was old—antiquated (See Hebrews 8:6-13; Galatians 4:21-31; II Corinthians 3:6ff).

LAMENTATIONS

Lamentations 1:7-The word "sabbath" (KJV) is better translated "desolations" (ASV) or an equivalent denoting Jerusalem's downfall.

Lamentations 2:6-The sabbath was no longer kept in Jerusalem because of her destruction (Jeremiah 17:21ff; cf Zephaniah 3:18).

EZEKIEL

Ezekiel 20:10-12 "V.10 So I caused them to go forth out of the land of Egypt, and brought them into the wilderness. V.11 And I gave them my statutes, and showed them mine ordinances, which if a man do, he shall live in them. V.12 Moreover also I gave them my sabbaths, to be a sign between me and them, that they might know that I am Jehovah that sanctifieth them."

GOOD POINTS

One: The sabbath was given to Israel—"them"—only (V.12, cf V.5ff).

Two: The sabbath was given unto Israel after they were "brought out of Egypt" and not before (V.10; See Deuteronomy 5:1-15-Two.2).

Three: The sabbath was given when the rest of the "statutes" and "ordinances" were given. (V.11). It was thus a part of the Sinaitic covenant, which covenant was done away (Ephesians 2:15).

Four: The sabbath was a "sign" between God and Israel

and no other nation (V.12,20: See Exodus 31:17f-One.2)

Ezekiel 20:13,16,20-24 — Israel's breaking of the sabbath in the wilderness pointed out.

Ezekiel 22:8 — Israel's profaning the sabbath denounced.

Ezekiel 22:26 "Her priests have done violence to my law, and have profaned my holy things: they have made no distinction between the holy and the common, neither have they caused men to discern between the unclean and the clean, and have hid their eyes from my sabbaths, and I am profaned among them."

ASSERTION: This verse perfectly describes ministers who profane the sabbath today.

ANSWER: This text has nothing in the world to do with the Christian Age or Christian ministers. (This, of course, is just the Sabbatarian's way of pronouncing judgment upon every preacher who isn't a Sabbatarian!) Ezekiel is describing the sins in Jerusalem, here specifically amongst the priests and princes, which led to her destruction in 586 BC (cf V.2,6,15f,18f,30f; Nehemiah 13:17ff). The Sabbatarian's unwarranted appeal to this text shows his real purpose in seeking to validate sabbath-keeping: he wants to bring in everything else from the old law which he holds to—even the ceremonial "clean and unclean." One minute he says the ceremonial law of Moses was that which was abolished at the cross (not the moral law of the decalogue), and the next minute he seeks to bind that same ceremonial law (cf Mark 7:19 for the abolishment of the "clean and unclean"; also Acts 10:15; I Timothy 4:3-5).

Ezekiel 23:38—Samaria (Oholah) and Jerusalem (Oholibah) punished for profaning the sabbath (V.4,36f).

Ezekiel 44:24 —Priests to keep sabbath in the new sanctuary. This temple vision is likely two-fold in application, dealing with the Jewish religious restoration in their return from captivity and symbolically typlifying the Christian church (See Isaiah 56:4-6 #2 for an explanation of two-fold prophecies).

Ezekiel 45:17—A list of the holy days (See Numbers 28:9; Colossians 2:16).

Ezekiel 46:1, 3f, 12—Worship at the gate on the sabbath. This is not the gate of the city. It is the gate of the inner court of the temple. This gate was operated just opposite of the city gate: it being opened on the sabbath and closed throughout the week; the city gate being opened throughout the week and closed on the sabbath (Nehemiah 13:19).

DANIEL

Daniel 7:25 "And he shall speak words against the Most High, and shall wear out the saints of the Most High; and he shall think to change the times and the law..."

ASSERTION: This is prophetic of how either the Roman Emperor, Constantine (AD 321), or the Roman Catholic pope (AD 364-Council of Laodicea) changed the sabbath "times" and the ten commandment"law."

ANSWER: This text has nothing to do with Constantine, the pope, the sabbath or the ten commandment law.

1. Constantine did not change the day of Christian assembly and worship (supposedly the Christian sabbath) from Saturday to Sunday; he merely issued an edict (of many other edicts favoring Christianity) declaring it lawful and acceptable for everyone (especially the pagans) to honor the day which Christians had always kept and were keeping at that time, Sunday (cf Mosheim, Century IV, Part 2, Ch.4, Section 5; Sozomen, Eccl. Hist., Bk.2, Ch.VIII, p.22). Several Roman emperors have been

set forth as the fulfillment of the "little **horn**" (V.8) or eleventh king (V.24), yet no king past Domitian harmonizes according to the historical interpretation of Daniel (cf"The Book of Daniel", Jim McGuiggan). (Notice that "Constantine" is not specifically named in this chapter.) Also, to say Constantine changed either the sabbath or the ten commandment law is to contradict the many New Testament passages which confirm that Christ abolished both hundreds of years before Constantine was born (See Revelation 1:10; Colossians 2:14-17; Hebrews 7:12; 8:6ff; 10:9).

2. A Roman pope (not mentioned either!) could not have changed the sabbath for many reasons: (a) No pope existed in AD364! Roman bishops did not exercise any special authority over other bishops for over 200 years after this council. (b) No one from the church in Rome—neither bishop nor delegate—attended the council of Laodicea (a small, local council held in a Greek city without Rome's knowledge-See Canright, pp.243-248). (c) To say this is the pope is to run contrary to the context which is definitely dealing with the fourth kingdom, including its kings, kingdoms and persecuting power. Such makes this a prophecy of the civil Roman government and not the Roman Catholic Church, which church did not actually come into full bloom until after the Roman government ceased its persecution of the saints! The popish interpretation of this text is according to the **hysterical** method of interpreting Daniel and not the **historical** (See Daniel 2:31-45; 8:20ff on the four civil empires). (d) To say this is the pope changing the sabbath is to contradict the recorded history of the Roman Catholic Church which makes no such claim (See Canright, pp. 210-214; 234-248). (e) To say this refers to the pope's changing the Christian's day of assembly from Saturday to Sunday is to contradict the many passages which say Christ did so over half a millennium before the first pope existed (See Revelation 1:10). (f) Even if the Cath-

olic church did lay claim to such a change, Christians would not be obligated to accept it. Nor are Christians obligated to believe such just because the Sabbatarian believes it. First, because the Catholic church is not our authority in religion; the New Testament is. Second, because even Sabbatarians do not accept any of the other outlandish claims made by the Roman church. They deny the Catholic Church's claim to being the only true church. They deny their claim that Peter was the first pope and that the pope is infallible. They deny their claim that the Roman church gave us the Bible, etc. The Sabbatarian tells us that all these claims are false, and then he wants us to believe the claim made by the same church concerning their change of the sabbath, which claim cannot be historically verified!

3. The word "sabbath" does not appear in this verse. The word "times" is not the word "sabbaths," and it very unlikely refers to religious times at all (cf Daniel 4:17,32; Genesis 18:14). It rather is in reference to ordained periods or seasons of time, i.e., as God, in his foreknowledge, ordains the length of time a king or kingdom shall stand (Daniel 2:21; Acts 17:26; cf Genesis 15:16). Also, as we have already shown how no Roman emperor or pope changed the sabbath, then the word "times" could not find fulfillment in such.

4. The words "ten commandment" do not appear before the word "law" in this verse. Nor can the word law, as used here, be confined to religious law. It refers to law in general, including statutes and decrees (cf Daniel 2:13,15; 6:9). Now the Roman emperors enacted many decrees, laws and interdicts (many which were wicked, oppressing and contrary to godliness), yet not one of them changed the sabbath law. Christ changed that one (Colossians 2:16)! And He certainly doesn't fit the description of the wicked one in this verse!

Thus the Sabbatarians read five words into this verse

which are not in it: Constantine, pope, sabbath, ten and commandment. (They actually read an entire theory into it!) All of these additions are contrary to the text and contradict the truth of God's word which says Christ abolished not only the sabbath but the entire law (Hebrews 7:12; 10:9).

HOSEA

Hosea 2:11 "I will also cause all her mirth to cease, her feasts, her new moons, and her sabbaths, and all her solemn assemblies."

COMMENT: This passage has been used by many opponents of sabbath-keeping, yet it is in no way a prophecy of the cessation of the sabbath at the cross (Colossians 2:16). Such is totally out of the historical context. This is a prophecy concerning the taking away of Israel (northern ten tribes) by the Assyrians. There, in captivity, they would not enjoy their religious freedom. The Assyrians would not allow thim to observe their holy days and rites (V.12; 9:1-5).

GOOD POINT: Notice that the sabbath was Israel's sabbath- "**her** sabbaths"- and no other nation's (See Deuteronomy 5:1-15; cf Mark 2:23-28).

JOEL
N/A

AMOS

Amos 8:5-9 "Saying, When will the new moon be gone, that we may sell grain? and the sabbath that we may set forth wheat, making the ephah small, and the shekel great, and dealing falsely with balances of deceit... V.9 And it shall come to pass in that day, saith the Lord Jehovah, that I will cause the sun to go down at noon, and I will darken the earth in the clear day."

COMMENT: Many also say this is a prophecy of the abrogation of the sabbath (V.5-which the Jews supposedly desired) at the cross (V.9-when the sun would be made to go down at noon, i.e., supposedly at the cross, Mark 15:33f). Yet this text has nothing to do with any such abrogation of the sabbath at the cross. First of all, it is untenable to think that the Jews, who gloried in all such external, distinguishing laws (laws which set them apart from other nations), were here requesting that their sabbath be abolished. Amos was rather pointing out their heartless observance of the sabbath: how they kept it only externally, mechanically or legalistically (Amos 5:21-23); how while in the very process of keeping it their hearts longed for it to be over that they might get back to their trading and money making (Ibid. 8:5b-6). Such trading was illegal on the sabbath day (Exodus 20:9f; Nehemiah 10:31; 13:15-22). **(Note:** The Jews, surviving unto the first century, had not changed from these attitudes towards religious observance and money-making. Yet they did find the solution to the problem. They just moved their businesses into the temple-John 2:13ff!). Secondly, God did not promise the end of the sabbath in verse nine; he promised the end of Israel, which, of course, would end her keeping sabbaths (Amos 8:2f,10-14; cf4:12; 5:2,6,18,27; 7:16f). The term "cause her sun to go down at noon" is symbolic of how God would overthrow Israel in her prime, in the midst of her prosperity–in the middle of her sunshiny day—when she'd at least expect it (cf Jeremiah 6:4; 15:8; Zephaniah 2:4 for the same term). One does not expect the sun to go down in the middle of the day. Yet one does not expect a nation to fall at the height of its glory either (as Israel, materialistically speaking, was when Amos wrote). Thus there seems to be no reason for making this a prophecy of the literal darkening at Calvary. It better applies to the dark days which were about to befall Israel. (Also, there seems to be no reason for assuming this is a two-fold prophecy.)

OBADIAH
N/A
JONAH
N/A
MICAH
N/A
NAHUM
N/A
HABAKKUK
N/A
ZEPHANIAH
N/A
HAGGAI
N/A
ZECHARIAH
N/A
MALACHI

Malachi 3:6- See comments at Hebrews 13:8.

MATTHEW

Matthew 5:17-19 "V.17 Think not that I came to destroy the law or the prophets: I came not to destroy, but to fulfill. V. 18 For verily I say unto you, Till heaven and earth pass away, one jot or one tittle shall in no wise pass away from the law, till all things be accomplished. V.19 Whosoever therefore shall break one of these least commandments, and shall teach men so, shall be called least in the kingdom of heaven. . . ."

ASSERTIONS

One: Christ didn't come to destroy (abolish) the ten commandment law, he came to fulfill (or enforce) it (Goodspeed; See Romans 3:31).

Two: If the word "fulfill" means to abolish as opponents of the sabbath assert, then Christ abolished all righteousness; for he "fulfilled all righteousness" in his baptism (Matthew 3:15)!

Three: Not one jot, tittle or least commandment (as the sabbath is least among so many so-called Christians) shall pass away from the ten commandments as long as the heavens and earth stand.

ANSWERS

One: This text cannot be limited to the ten commandments.

1. For there is no mention of the words "ten commandments" in this text. To read such in is pure assumption. (a) We have already established the fact that the term "the law" refers to the entire law of Moses and not just to the Decalogue (See Deuteronomy 31:24-26). The rest of Christ's discourse in Matthew five (V. 21-48) also bears out this fact. He continued his discussion of the law which would not pass away and included laws not found in the Decalogue. He spoke of "swearing" (V.33; cf Leviticus 19:12) and "an eye for an eye" (V.38; cf Leviticus 24:20). These are found in the law of Moses. Thus, according to Sabbatarians, none of the laws of Moses have passed away. Even they deny such. (b) Also, this text does not deal with just the fulfilling of "the law" but includes "the prophets" (V.17). Now the Jews understood the term "the law and the prophets" as the entire Old Testament: "the law" being the five books of Moses; "the prophets" being the other inspired writings (Matthew 7:12; 11:13; 22:40; Luke 16:16, 29,31; John 1:45; Acts 7:42; 13:15; 24:14; 26:22; 28:23; Romans 3:21; See Luke 24:44 where the entire Old Testament is called the **"law of Moses**, prophets and Psalms. Yet the Psalms could also be considered under the pro-

phets, for David, the writer of most of the Psalms, was also a prophet - Acts 2:29f). Thus, according to the Sabbatarians, we are bound to keep every jot, tittle and least command of the entire Old Testament. Every jot and tittle of it must be **enforced**, including every command to offer animal sacrifices, build altars and temples, etc. Such is false, and how dare the Sabbatarians seek to bring Christians under the yoke/the enforcement of the Old Testament (Acts 15:5,10).

2. The word "fulfill" (V.17 - Gk. Pleroo) is not best translated as "enforced" but rather to relate the idea of filling up, bringing to pass, to completion, to accomplishment, to consummation or fulfillment (Thayer; See Standard Translations: KJV, ASV, RSV, NASV, NEB).[1] That this is the best translation here is further borne out in verse eighteen, which verse further explains verse seventeen, wherein our Lord used another Greek word (Ginomai) also translated as "fulfilled," which means to be accomplished, to come to pass or to be **fulfilled**. Things so fulfilled need only be fulfilled once and never again, nor do they need further establishing, enforcing, etc. (See Matthew 1:22f; 2:15, 17, 23; 4:14; Mark 1:15; John 7:8; Acts 14:26 for Pleroo; Luke 21:32 for Ginomai). Thus, though Christ did not come to abolish the law, he did, by bringing about total fulfillment or completion, bring about its consummation.

3. Romans 3:31 - See comments at that passage.

Two: Christ's being baptized of John (Matthew 3:15) was a necessary step in his fulfilling all the Father's righteous

---

1. It seems to be the conspicuous practice of radical religionists and sectarians to choose the less reliable, often spurious translations to back up their beliefs. If they cannot find one which agrees in word with their erroneous beliefs, they simply devise their own translation (See this writer's book "The Prejudices and Perversions of The New World Translation").

will — his appointed work (John 17:4) — concerning his earthly life and ministry. It was at his baptism that the Father had chosen to declare his Sonship (Matthew 3:16f; John 1:33f). Also, it was there that Christ would further exemplify his role as the humble and obedient Servant (Philippians 2:8; Hebrews 5:8). Once Jesus accomplished this particular righteous act, then it never needed to be accomplished or fulfilled again. Having so fulfilled this righteous act, we can say he abolished the need to do it again. Neither did he enforce the need for all others to be baptized for the same righteous purposes. For men are baptized for entirely different purposes than was Christ. Men are now baptized for forgiveness of sins and not to declare their righteousness (Acts 2:38; See this writer's book "There Has Always Been One Baptism"). Thus Christ's completion of this aspect of manifesting his righteousness (it would have been unrighteous for him to disobey any command of God) has nothing to do with abolishing God's righteous will concerning us.

Three: This text does not say that one jot, tittle or least commandment of the "ten commandments" shall not pass away as long as the heavens and earth remain.

1. Again, where does it say not one jot or tittle shall pass away from the "ten commandment" law? The words "ten commandment" are not even in the text! Also, which one of the ten commandments was less than the others (V.19)? This, without a doubt, refers to the entire law of Moses. Thus, again, according to the Sabbatarian's interpretation, we would be bound to keep every jot and tittle of the entire old law until the end of time. Such is false.

2. This doesn't say the law would not pass away as long as the heavens and earth remain; it says the heavens and earth would not pass away before—"till"—the law was completely accomplished, fulfilled or brought to

pass (Ginomai is the root of the word used, cf Luke 16:17). (a) Thus the law was to last until it was completely fulfilled. The question I pose to Sabbatarians is what part—jot or tittle—of the law did Christ fail to fulfill or accomplish? He fulfilled the full requirement of the law—sinless perfection (Galatians 3:10; Hebrews 4:15; I Peter 2:22). He thus provided the perfect sacrifice for sin that the law demanded (Hebrews 10:1-14). If he thus fulfilled it **all**, then it **all** passed away! (b) The law was not to be established as binding after it was so fulfilled. It was not to remain in force "till" it was filled full and then continue on as really established because of Christ's final approval. The entire old law had been fully established as a binding covenant since Sinai (Exodus 24:7f; cf Hebrews 9:17-20). It needed no further confirmation (Luke 16:31; cf Galatians 3:15; Hebrews 2:2). Also, the word "till" does not support the continuing of that which was fulfilled after it was fulfilled. The word "till' stands as the culmination point between the full fulfillment of the law and its passing away. Other passages where the word "till" is used confirm this to be true: "And (Joseph) knew her not **till** she had brought forth a son" (Matthew 1:25). Did Joseph continue his not knowing her after she had a son? (A Roman Catholic assertion.) "This generation shall not pass away, **till** all things be accomplished" (Luke 21:32). Did that generation continue on as an established generation after all things were accomplished? (They were all accomplished in that generation; the generation did pass away. See this writer's book "Second Peter Three Jewish Calamity or Universal Climax?") "The Jews banded together, and bound themselves under a curse, saying that they would neither eat nor drink **till** they had killed Paul" (Acts 23:12). Did these Jews plan to continue their fast after they had killed Paul? Absurd. Thus the law was to last "till" it was fulfilled and then pass away. Indeed it passed away, for it lasted "till" the new law of faith came and no longer (Galatians 3:19-25)!

Matthew 11:28-30 "Come unto me, all ye that labor and are heavy laden, and I will give you rest. Take my yoke upon you, and learn of me; for I am meek and lowly in heart: and ye shall find rest unto your souls. For my yoke is easy, and my burden is light."

GOOD POINT: Christ is the Christian's sabbath. The Christian church was not given a different physical sabbath day, replacing the Jews' seventh-day sabbath with a first-day sabbath. The physical sabbath day was not changed to another day; it was abolished altogether as a practice for God's people. The Christian has instead of a physical day to rest on a person to rest in, Jesus Christ! As all the physical Old Testament types were replaced with spiritual New Testament antitypes, so was the sabbath day: the Jew was delivered from the physical bondage of Egypt into the physical land of Canaan to rest on the physical sabbath day (Deuteronomy 5:15); the Christian was delivered from the spiritual bondage of sin and satan into the spiritual body/kingdom of Christ to enjoy spiritual rest continuously (Matthew 11:28ff; John 8:32-36; Colossians 1:13). Thus it is unscriptural to speak about any Christian sabbath day, Saturday or Sunday!

Matthew 12:1-4 - Christ's so-called violation of the sabbath by plucking corn to eat (See Mark 2:23-28). It must be understood that Jesus was no revolutionary, breaking the old law when he saw fit, for he kept the law perfectly. It was the man-made traditions and opinions (which were usually contrary to the true law) that he often disregarded.

Matthew 12:5 "Or have ye not read in the law that on the sabbath day the priests in the temple profane the sabbath and are guiltless?''

GOOD POINT: The Old Testament priests did not keep the **rest** of the sabbath in the temple. They continued to perform their priestly duties, i.e., they worked (Leviticus 24:8; Numbers 28:9f; I Chronicles 9:32). Now the temple served as a type of the church. It was God's dwelling place in Israel (I Kings 8:11,13, 29f). It was where the priests of Israel carried out their religious activities every day. Now the church, the antitype, is God's temple—his dwelling place (I Corinthians 3:16; Ephesians 2:21f; I Timothy 3:15). All Christians are priests serving in this spiritual temple, daily offering up spiritual sacrifices (I Peter 2:5). Thus, as the Old Testament priests did not have to observe the sabbath in the temple, so there is no keeping of sabbath in the church (the universal temple) by Christians (priests).

Matthew 12:8—Jesus was the lord of the sabbath (See: Mark 2:23-28).

Matthew 12:10-12 - It was always lawful to do things necessary and good on the sabbath. Many of the sabbath regulations and prohibitions were man-made and contrary to God's love and concern for man and his well-being (cf Matthew 15:9; 23:4). This text shows how a sheep's life was more important than strict adherence to even those divinely given sabbath ordinances.

Matthew 17:4f "And Peter answered, and said unto Jesus, Lord, it is good for us to be here: if thou wilt, I will make here three tabernacles; one for thee, and one for Moses, and one for Elijah. While he was yet speaking, behold, a bright cloud overshadowed them: and behold, a voice out of the cloud, saying, This is my beloved Son, in whom I am well pleased; hear ye him.''

GOOD POINT: We must hear Christ and not Moses, Joseph Smith, Ellen G. White, etc (cf Matthew 28:18; John 1:17; II Corinthians 3:15f). We must only include in Christ's new covenant that which he specifically authorized through his apostles and not everything not specifically abrogated from the Old Testament (John 13:20; 16:13; I Corinthians 2:16; 9:21; 14:37; Galatians 6:2).

Matthew 19:16-22 "V.16 And behold, one came to him and said, Teacher, what good thing shall I do, that I may have eternal life? V.17 And he said unto him, Why askest thou me concerning that which is good? One there is who is good: but if thou wouldest enter into life, keep the commandments. V.18 He saith unto him, Which? And Jesus said, Thou shalt not kill, Thou shalt not commit adultery, Thou shalt not steal, Thou shalt not bear false witness. V.19 Honor thy father and thy mother; and Thou shalt love thy neighbor as thyself. V.20 The young man saith unto him, All these things have I observed: What lack I yet? V.21 Jesus said unto him, If thou wouldest be perfect, go, sell that which thou hast, and give to the poor, and thou shalt have treasure in heaven: and come, follow me. V.22 But when the young man heard the saying, he went away sorrowful; for he was one that had great possessions."

ASSERTION: We can only have eternal life if we keep the ten commandments. Jesus even quoted five of them (V.18) to show that the Decalogue was under consideration and not the law of Moses.

ANSWER: This text does not teach eternal life is to be

obtained by commandment keeping, is not applicable to Christians and is not limited to the Decalogue.

1. No one, not even the most pious Jew, ever merited eternal life by keeping any set of commandments, not even the ten commandments. (They brought death not life - Romans 7:9f; II Corinthians 3:7). The only way the Jew could inherit eternal life by keeping commandments (apart from faith) was to keep all the commandments given in the Old Testament and not just ten of them. This he had to do perfectly throughout his entire adult life (Leviticus 18:5; Roman 10:5; Galatians 3:10-12). This brings to light the real point of our Lord in so answering this young legalist. For he could not "do" (V.16) enough to merit life, for he would never be able to keep the whole law perfectly (Romans 3:9,23; 4:1ff; cf Luke 17:10). Thus he needed something besides commandments to perfect and save him; he needed to have faith in Christ (V.21—which his renouncing all and following would have manifested). This the legalist did not have. He rather held to his law-keeping for justification and thus forfeited eternal life (John 5:39f). Yet, according to Sabbatarians, he should have been saved already, for he said he had kept the commandments (V.20 - the Sabbatarian says this is confined to just the ten commandments), which keeping Sabbatarians say is proof of one's salvation (See Revelation 7:2-4; 12:17). Jesus said more than law-keeping was needed to perfect (V.21).

2. This young man lived under the old covenant before Christ's new covenant was ratified (Hebrews 8:6-13; 9:15ff). He was therefore obligated to keep all the commandments of the Old Testament, including the ten commandments. But we, on this side of Calvary, are not so obligated.

3. This text cannot be limited to the ten commandments. First, the Lord did not say that this young man needed

to keep just the "ten commandments." The words aren't in the text. He said he needed to keep the "commandments." Now anyone can look up the word "commandments" and see it cannot be limited to the Decalogue (See Genesis 26:5#1-2). Also, Jesus made this very clear by including a "commandment" not found in the ten commandments but rather in the so-called ceremonial law of Moses (V. 19 - "Thou shalt love thy neighbor as thyself" - cf Matthew 22:36-40; Leviticus 19:18). Now, if Jesus' quoting a portion of the ten commandments means he was binding **on us** (today) the keeping of the entire Decalogue to inherit eternal life, then his quoting a portion of the Mosaical law would mean he also bound **all** of it upon us as well. Must we really keep the entire old law—the Decalogue and law of Moses—to have eternal life? If so, then why doesn't the Sabbatarian do so? Actually, the quoting of a portion or a law does not automatically bind the whole; it only binds that specifically stated. Paul quoted a portion of the Mosaical law in I Corinthians 9:9, yet he did not therefore bring over into the new covenant as binding the entire old law. He only bound that specifically stated. Thus, technically speaking, this text in Matthew nineteen cannot be used as authority for binding the sabbath command, not only because it occurred before the new covenant was ratified, but also because the sabbath command is not specifically stated in the text! (If this young man would have lived today and asked his question of a Sabbatarian, then he would have been told: "First of all, Thou shalt keep the sabbath day holy!" Of course, remember, this young man lived under the entire old law and had to keep the sabbath. Yet I wonder why Jesus did not exalt the keeping of such? Could it have been because the sabbath command was nigh unto vanishing away? ? ?)

Matthew 22:36-40 "V.36 Teacher, which is the great commandment in the law? V.37 And he said unto him, Thou shalt love thy Lord thy God with all thy heart, and with all thy soul, and with all thy mind. V.38 This is the great and first commandment. V.39 And a second like unto it is this, Thou shalt love thy neighbor as thyself. V.40 On these two commandments the whole law hangeth, and the prophets."

GOOD POINT: All the Old Testament Law hangs on these two greatest of commands. The Sabbatarian maintains that only the ceremonial law of Moses was abolished at Calvary and the ten commandments alone continued on. Yet these two greatest of commandments appear in the so-called ceremonial section of the Mosaical law and not in the Decalogue (Leviticus 19:18; Deuteronomy 6:5)! This, according to them, was abolished. Thus, by their own admission, the Decalogue was also abolished, for it (being part of the "whole law") hung on these two great commands found in that which was abolished, the law of Moses. Thus all of the law—Moses and the Decalogue—fell at the same time.

Matthew 24:20 "And pray ye that your flight be not in the winter, neither on a sabbath."

ASSERTIONS

One: The sabbath was still to be considered holy in AD70. Christians were here told to pray that they would not have to violate or desecrate it by traveling—taking "flight"—on it.

Two: This is proof that the sabbath would be a part of the new covenant. Here Christians were told to keep it for forty years after the new covenant had been ratified.

ANSWERS

One: This does not say Christians would desecrate the sabbath by traveling on it.

1. Where in this text does it say they were to pray that they would not violate or desecrate the sabbath? Such is not in the text and is pure assumption. Such is also entirely wrong, for even if Christians would have been obligated to keep the sabbath day holy, they would not have been guilty of any violation or desecration if they would have traveled on it. First of all, where is travel forbidden on the sabbath? Sabbatarians say all the old ordinances, except for the Decalogue, were nailed to the cross; then they seek to bind restrictions not found in either the Decalogue or the New Testament! Secondly, our Lord made it quite plain that sabbath regulations were not to be imposed upon one at the expense of his well-being (See Matthew 12:10-12; Mark 2:23-28). Yet the Sabbatarian would have our Lord telling his beloved disciples that it would be better for them to lose their lives in the overthrow of Jerusalem than to desecrate a man-made ordinance! How utterly false!

2. That this prayerful precaution was given for safety and not religious reasons is obvious from the context. (a) The other precautions were for safety and not religious reasons:"not in winter" and "not give suck" (V.19). (b) Travel on the sabbath would have been difficult and dangerous. The gates of the city of Jerusalem would likely be closed, making departure nigh unto impossible (See Nehemiah 13:15-22; Jeremiah 17:27). (The open gate of Ezekiel 46:1 was not one of the outer city gates but one of the inner courts of the temple.) The fanatical Jews, who constantly sought to kill Christ for so-called violations of their sabbath, would kill those seeking to make such a burdensome exodus on their sabbath. They restricted travel to approximately one mile on the sabbath (Acts 1:12), and such would not be sufficient to escape the seige. Also, lodging places and stables would be closed on the sabbath. Thus those es-

capees would not be able to find shelter or beasts of burden to help on their journey unto safety. This would make a winter departure (on the sabbath) especially hazardous.

Note: Some feel the Jewish Christians would still offend their consciences if they had to do such moving on the sabbath. Many were quite conscientious concerning their Jewish and national customs for some time after Calvary, but I personally do not see this problem being dealt with in this precaution (cf Acts 21:17-26).

Two: This text does not say the sabbath was to be a part of the new covenant nor that Christians would be keeping it in AD 70.

1. Where is the sabbath commanded for **Christians** to keep? It isn't. Where is there one sabbath regulation in the New Testament? One violation condemned? One rebuked for failure to keep it? One charge to keep it? One punishment for not keeping it? The Old Testament is replete with such commands, charges, admonishments, etc., yet such is nowhere to be found in the New Testament. The only logical explanation for this absence is that the sabbath was no longer binding. Also, the only mention of the sabbath in the New Testament, as far as the Christian is concerned, is that telling him not to allow anyone to bind it upon him (Colossians 2:16)!

2. Where is there a mention of Christians keeping the sabbath as a holy day after Pentecost? See Acts passages for refutations of asserted passages.) It is true that Jewish Christians may have kept the sabbath for some time after Pentecost (according to uninspired history); yet they only kept it as a national custom, as they observed many other Jewish customs (Acts 16:3; 21:17-26), and they also kept the first day of the week as the day of Christian assembly and worship—it being the Christian's holy day, the Lord's day (See Revelation 1:10).

Matthew 28:1 "Now late on the sabbath day, as it began to dawn toward the first day of the week, came Mary Magdalene and the other Mary to see the sepulchre."

ASSERTIONS

One: Sunday is not the true sabbath. This says the true sabbath was before the first day.

Two: If Saturday ceased to be the sabbath day at the cross, then why did Matthew, a Christian writing years after the cross, still call the seventh day the "sabbath day?"

ANSWERS

One: It is true that the true sabbath was on Saturday and before the first day, Sunday. Such I care not to dispute. No student of the Word has ever maintained that the sabbath was changed from Saturday to Sunday. (Only Sabbatarians use such lingo). Sunday is not a sabbath (rest) day. Christians are not required to keep any sabbath days, seventh-day or otherwise (Colossians 2:16).

Two: Matthew's calling the seventh day the sabbath day does not mean he recognized it as an authorized day for Christian observance. The sabbath day ceased only as far as Christians were concerned. The Jews continued to keep it, as they do even unto this day. Thus it was entirely natural to call the seventh day what it had been called for centuries, the sabbath day. (I often call it the sabbath day (of Jews), and I certainly do not believe I have to keep it!) The Christian writers referred to all the Jewish rites, things, customs and days by their established Jewish designations: "sabbath day's journey (Acts 1:12), "Pentecost" (Ibid. 2:1; 20:16), "days of unleavened bread" (Ibid. 12:3), "synagogue" (Ibid. 13:43), "circumcision" (Ibid. 16:3), etc. Yet their calling them such did not mean they honored them as Christian ordinances. They most certainly did not. Even Sabbatarians do not believe all these mentioned are Christian ordinances (See Luke 23:56)!

MARK

Mark 1:21 "And they go into Capernaum; and straightway on the sabbath day he entered into the synagogue and taught."

ASSERTION: Jesus always kept the sabbath. It was his continual custom (Luke 4:16). We are to walk in his steps (I Peter 2:21; I John 2:6). Thus, if we would follow Christ, then we must keep the sabbath as he did.

ANSWER: We do not have to do everything Jesus did in order to be his followers.

1. Jesus was born under the authority of the Old Testament law and was thus obligated to keep it (Galatians 4:4). We are not under the old law and are not thus obligated to keep it (Romans 6:14f; cf Galatians 4:21-31).

2. Jesus kept all the Mosaical law (not just the ten commandments), including all the holy days, rites and ceremonies: He was circumcised (Luke 2:21f); he kept the Passover (Luke 2:41f; 22:1,7ff); he kept the feast of tabernacles (John 7:2-10); etc. Do Sabbatarians insist that we must keep all these as Jesus did in order to walk in his steps? If so, thon they themselves are on a detour, for they do not keep but a small portion of what Jesus kept! (They are on many detours from the New Testament pattern of Christianity!) It was also Christ's **custom** to enter into the synagogue on the sabbath. Must we go to the Jewish synagogues on the sabbath? They have no case!

Mark 2:23-28 "V.23 And it came to pass, that he was going on the sabbath day through the grainfields; and his disciples began, as they went,

> to pluck the ears. V.24 And the Pharisees said unto him, Behold, why do they on the sabbath day that which is not lawful: V.25 And he said unto them, Did ye never read what David did, when he had need, and was hungry, he, and they that were with him? V. 26 How he entered into the house of God when Abiathar was high priest, and ate the showbread, which it is not lawful to eat save for the priests, and gave also to them that were with him? V.27 And he said unto them, The sabbath was made for man, and not man for the sabbath: V.28 so that the Son of man is lord even of the sabbath."

ASSERTIONS

One: This says the sabbath was made for all mankind and not just for the Jews (V.27). It is obvious also that there are health reasons behind sabbath-keeping which apply to all men and not just to the Jews (all men need rest).

Two: The sabbath is the "lord's day" of Revelation 1:10, for this says Christ is the Lord of it (V. 28). Indeed he's the Lord of it, for he made it (cf Exodus 20:10).

ANSWERS

One: This text does not say the sabbath was made for **all mankind**, for all nations, all flesh or for all the world (the word"all" is not in the text) as do other universal texts (See Matthew 28:19; Mark 16:16; John 3:16; Acts 2:17; Titus 2:11; I Timothy 2:4).

1. We know the sabbath was made for only one race and nation, the Jews of Israel (See Deuteronomy 5:1-15; Hosea 2:11). Sabbatarians have yet to present one passage showing where God gave the sabbath to any nation other than Israel. It is quite obvious that the Lord is only thinking of Jews in his use of the term "man"

in this text, for all the characters mentioned were Jews (V.24-26-"Pharisees, David, Abiathar, priests"). Also, in many other places the generic word "man" (Gk. Anthropos) is used in reference to Jews only: all the Jews called "O man" (Romans 2:1,3; cf 3:1); Judas, definitely a Jew, is referred to just as a "man" (Mark 14:21); the Jews circumcised a "man" (John 7:22); the law of Moses judged a "man" (John 7:51). Thus just because Jesus did not say the sabbath was made for Jewish mankind does not mean it wasn't; and his saying it was made for "man" could not mean it was made for all mankind when His Bible says it was only made for Israel!

2. Where does the Bible say the sabbath was given for health reasons? The Bible says it was given for religious and not health reasons (Exodus 16:28f; 20:8-11; 31:16f; Deuteronomy 5:15). Why would resting on the seventh day be any healthier than resting on any other day? It isn't! Actually, this text, if it teaches anything about the sabbath in relation to man's health, teaches that sabbath-keeping can be detrimental to man's health if pressed upon man under every circumstance (V.25f). Indeed Sabbatarians have been guilty of enforcing sabbath-keeping to the detriment of not a few's well-being!

3. Also, this text shows how the sabbath was not a moral command kept by man from the beginning, for it had to be made. (It was made in Exodus 16-20.) Notice this text does not say it was made for man from the "beginning," as was marriage (cf Matthew 19:4ff). Which other command of the ten commandments had to be made moral later? The other nine were intrinsically right from the beginning, reflecting God's revealed, righteous nature, will and desire for man – created in his moral image — to be holy as He is holy (I Peter 1: 15f. See Exodus 20:8–11 - Two, 2). Which command, other than the sabbath, is lower than man and subject to being set aside

under certain circumstances? When, or under what circumstances, can man lawfully commit adultery? Obviously, never! Man's life is not above God's holy and moral laws. Yet even a sheep's life is more important than rigid enforcement of the sabbath (Matthew 12:10-12)!

Two: This text does not say the sabbath day is the "Lord's day" of Revelation 1:10, nor does it remotely imply such.

1. Christ's pointing out his lordship over the sabbath was not for the purpose of pointing to his establishment of the sabbath as a holy day (its origin), nor was he then ordaining it to be the Lord's day. He was rather, as any unbiased student of the word can easily see, pointing out his right to regulate the sabbath. If the sabbath could be set aside by mere men under certain circumstances (the sabbath being made for man and not he for it), then surely the "Son of man" (head of all men) could set it aside when necessary to further or continue his earthly ministry. (In this case, they needed to eat to continue following Christ-cf Mark 6:31-44.) He thus had the right to regulate it to accomplish things more important, such as his ministering life to all men. Now, since he had the right to regulate it, then he also had the right to abolish it (Colossians 2:16). If he could not abolish something he was Lord of, as Sabbatarians assert, then he would not have been its lord, it would have been his! Yet, as he was the lord of the Passover and abolished it (Exodus 12:11), so his being lord of the sabbath meant he could abolish it. (Even Sabbatarians admit the Passover was abolished.)

2. The sabbath is never referred to as the "Lord's day" in the Bible or by the Jews (See Revelation 1:10). Only modern-day Sabbatarians erroneously assert such.

Mark 3:2,4—Doing good was always lawful on the sabbath

(See Matthew 12:10-12).

Mark 6:2—Jesus kept the sabbath (See Mark 1:21).

Mark 15:42-The Preparation day was Friday, the day before the sabbath (cf Luke 23:54). The contention of some that Christ arose on Saturday is refuted by the fact that he died on the "Preparation day," meaning "Friday" in modern Greek. The third day from Friday, according to Jewish reckoning (a part of a day was considered as a whole - cf Esther 4:16; 5:1), would be Sunday and not Saturday (See Norman F. Douty, "Another Look at Seventh-Day Adventism," p. 81. footnote 58).

Mark 16:1f-Assertion: That the true sabbath, or day of rest, remained to be Saturday (and not Sunday) even after Christ's death is seen by the postponement of the burial procedures (work) from Saturday until Sunday (See Matthew 28:1; Luke 23:56).

LUKE

Luke 4:16,31—See Mark 1:21

Luke 6:1,2,5—See Mark 2:23-28

Luke 6:6f,9—See Matthew 12:10-12

Luke 13:10—See Mark 1:21

Luke 13:14-16—See Matthew 12:10-12

Luke 14:1,3,5—See Matthew 12:10-12

Luke 23:54—See Mark 15:42

Luke 23:56 "And they returned, and prepared spices and ointments. And on the sabbath they rested according to the commandment."

ASSERTION: This passage proves the seventh-day sabbath was not abolished at the cross, for here we find the disciples keeping it after the crucifixion. The sabbath is therefore a part of Christ's new covenant which was ratified at the cross (Hebrews 9:15-17).

ANSWER: This passage does not say the disciples kept the sabbath according to the new covenant; it says they kept it according to the "commandment," which commandment is found in the Old Testament law of Moses and not in that recorded after Calvary. That this is so can be seen by several other facts:

1. The Spirit had not yet been given to guide the apostles into all truth (John 7:39; 14:26; 16:12f). They therefore were not correct in all their beliefs and practices at this point of time. They did not understand the death of Jesus much less the many consequences of his death: his abolishing the old law, ratifying the new law, fully atoning for sins, destroying the power of Satan in it, etc. (Luke 24:17-21,25). They were not enlightened unto these fulfillments in Christ's death until after the resurrection (Luke 24:27,32,44f; See Acts 10:9-48 for further enlightenment of Peter). Thus they did not know Christ had fulfilled the old law and ratified the new law in his death (See Matthew 5:17-19). Therefore, it was only natural that they would still be keeping the sabbath (as part of the old law) before they were enlightened concerning its being done away in Christ's death (Colossians 2:14-16).

2. These same disciples kept the day of Pentecost some seven weeks after this occasion (Acts 2:1). Must we keep it also? If so, then why don't Sabbatarians keep it? Thus just because the disciples did something (sometimes ignorantly, sometimes out of custom) does not automatically make it a part of Christ's new covenant.

3. Where is the sabbath commanded in the new covenant administered by Christ's apostles, his holy ambassadors? Jesus said they would be guided into all truth when the Spirit would come and empower them (John 16:12f). This he did on Pentecost (Acts 2:1ff). The apostles then proceeded to reveal **all the truth** (Acts 20:20,27; Jude 3,17). Yet where have they commanded the keeping of the sabbath? They haven't. The only truth they revealed

about the sabbath concerns its abolishment (Colossians 2:16; cf also Romans 14:5f; Galatians 4:10)! The sabbath is not a part of the new covenant!

Luke 24:47-The new covenant sprang forth from Jerusalem and not Sinai (Acts 1:8; Galatians 4:21-31; cf Isaiah 2:3; Micah 4:2). This includes the gospel being preached first from physical Jerusalem on Pentecost (Acts 2) and continuing forever from spiritual Jerusalem, the church (Galatians 4:26; I Timothy 3:15; Hebrews 12:18ff).

JOHN

John 5:9-18-Notice the ridiculous regulations of the Jews concerning the sabbath. A man, having been cured of a thirty eight year crippling infirmity, was rebuked for taking up his bed (pad) and walking!

John 5:16,18-Jesus being persecuted for his supposed sabbath violations. Of course, Jesus never broke any of the divine decrees concerning the sabbath or any other matter (John 8:46).

John 7:22f-Notice the inconsistencies of the Jewish reglations concerning the sabbath. One could be mutilated-as in circumcision-on the sabbath, but he could not be made whole.

John 9:14,16-The accusation of the Jews that Christ was a sinner because he healed on the sabbath was actually denied by the God-given power he displayed (John 9:31-33; 10:37f).

John 19:31-The bodies of crucified victims, according to Jewish law, were not to hang on the cross over night, especially on the sabbath (Deuteronomy 21:22f). Yet notice the hypocrisy of the Jews in this matter. They would not dare violate one of their sabbath regulations which were more important than life to them (Mark 2:23–28), but they had no qualms whatsoever about killing an innocent man (cf Matthew 23:23f)! Notice a similar act of hypocrisy in

John 18:28, where they are found breaking the law in their trial of an innocent man (no evidence, false witnesses), yet they would not enter into the Praetorium because they did not want to defile themselves that they might eat the Passover! They were really rotten inside (Matthew 23:27).

ACTS

Acts 1:12-"Sabbath day's journey" (approxiamately 2,000 paces, or one mile).

Acts 13:14—"But they (Paul and company), passing through from Perga, came to Antioch of Pisidia; and they went into the synagogue on the sabbath day, and sat down."

ASSERTION: The apostles and early disciples kept the sabbath long after the church was established and the New Testament was in force. Thus sabbath-keeping was a Christian practice.

ANSWER: This text (and no other text) does not say the apostles or the disciples kept the sabbath or that it was a Christian practice.

1. Everything about this assembly shows it was a Jewish assembly and not a Christian assembly: they were in **a synagogue** (V.14); they were reading the **law and the prophets** (V.15), which would be the Old Testament scriptures, the law of Moses, and not the New Testament (V.39; cf 17:2,11); they were Jewish **rulers of the synagogue** (V.15); they were **men of Israel**, thus Jews (V.16), and those that **feared God**, likely meaning proselytes of the gate, i.e., uncircumcised Gentiles who believed in Jehovah and adhered to many of the laws of the Old Testament (V.16; cf 10:2f; 8:27); and Paul preached their **Jewish history** unto them (V.17-29). Thus Paul's purpose for going to this synagogue on the sabbath was not to assemble with Christians in a Christian assem-

bly (for no Christians other than Paul and his company were present, only Jews and proselytes-V.43,46) but to teach those of the Jewish religion. When else would he find them assembled to study things religious? (Many Jews were like many "church-goers" today: "Once a week will do" - V42; cf Amos 8:5). Now, just because Paul assembled with those of the Jewish religion on their sabbath day for teaching purposes, does not mean he was keeping the sabbath as a Christian practice, any more than if I assembled with Seventh-day Adventists on Saturday (to teach or debate) would mean I was keeping the sabbath as a Christian practice. I have so assembled and I assure you I was not keeping the sabbath! Also, the early disciples assembled in the temple daily. Yet does such mean they believed all days were sanctified days (Acts 2:46)? Certainly not. And, further, must we also enter Jewish synagogues as they did? If so, then why don't Sabbatarians do so? Must we also keep the day of Pentecost as many of the early Christians (Jewish) did (Acts 2:1; 20:16; I Corinthians 16:8f)? If so, then why don't Sabbatarians keep it? Paul did! Now, we know, because the Bible tells us so, that Paul kept or used such sabbaths, feast days and customs in order to gain an advantage in evangelism—to reach the masses of the Jews—and not because he believed in keeping part of the old covenant or that such things were demanded in the new covenant (See Acts 16:3; 21:20-26-for other Jewish practices kept for expedience sake; cf I Corinthians 9:20-22-for the principle). **Note:** Anyone may keep the sabbath or any other day, as did Paul, as long as he does not bind it as a New Testament religious requirement or law (See Acts 18:4-11).

2. The New Testament nowhere commands Christians to keep the sabbath. It does tell them, though, not to allow anyone to bind it upon them (Colossians 2:16). It is therefore most definitely not a Christian practice.

Acts 13:27-The prophets, as was Moses (Acts 15:21), were read every sabbath. Thus the Jews were without excuse for not discerning Christ to be the Messiah, for they all wrote concerning him (John 5:39f, 46f; Acts 3:18-24).

Acts 13:42-44 "And as they went out, they besought that these words might be spoken to them the next sabbath. Now when the synagogue broke up, many of the Jews and of the devout proselytes followed Paul and Barnabas; who, speaking to them, urged them to continue in the grace of God. And the next sabbath almost the whole city was gathered together to hear the word of God."

ASSERTION: This shows that Gentile Christians, here referred to a "devout proselytes," kept the sabbath.

ANSWER: Christians are not called "proselytes" in the Bible! The "devout proselytes" spoken of here refers to Gentiles who had espoused the Jewish faith and not the Christian faith (See comments on verse 14; cf Matthew 23:15; Acts 2:10; 15:1ff; 18:4; Thayer on Proselutos). None of these, neither the Jews nor the Gentile proselytes, had yet obeyed Paul's gospel. They, then, were not Christians! Notice their conversion: Paul preached to them (V.16-41); they wanted to hear more (V.42); the Jews rejected the gospel, and the Gentile proselytes, including, perhaps, other Gentiles in the city who came, accepted (V.44-48). Thus this is not an example of Gentile Christians keeping the sabbath, as the Gentiles were not Christians at the time they are seen meeting in the synagogue on the sabbath. The keeping of sabbath by Jews and Gentile proselytes to the Jewish faith is not authority for what Christians must do!

Acts 15:19-21 "Wherefore my judgment is, that we trouble not them that from among the Gentiles turn to God; but that we write unto them, that they abstain from the pollutions of idols, and

> from fornication, and from what is strangled, and from blood. For Moses from generations of old hath in every city them that preach him, being read in the synagogues every sabbath."

ASSERTION: This shows that not even all of the ceremonial law was abolished at the cross, much less all of the Decalogue. In fact, only that of the Old Testament which was specifically pointed out as abolished in the New Testament is not binding.

ANSWER: This is not the binding upon Christians, Gentile or Jew, a part of the old Mosaical law for the following reasons:

1. The apostles had just sternly defended the Gentile Christian's liberty from all the Mosaical law (V.1-19). They certainly would not then turn right around and bind them under a part of it (Galatians 2:14; Colossians 2:14-16), especially since to bind them under one part would be to bind them under it all and cause them to fall from grace (Galatians 3:10; 5:3f)!

(a) that which was here bound upon the Gentiles was a prohibition of their exercising their Christian liberty (to eat all meats) at the expense of offending the Jews (who would be offended at their eating of such sacrificial and bloody meats-V.21,29) and of their past pagan, idolatrous practices, of which fornication was common in the performance of many of the religious ceremonies. Thus Gentiles were not here being asked to obey a part of the Mosaical code. But they were rather being asked to respect the customs and religious beliefs of the Jews (who studied Moses every sabbath) with whom they lived and to keep themselves pure from idols (V.21; 21:20ff). These are Christians principles and not enforcements of Mosaical laws (Romans 14:14-23; I Corinthians 8:7-13; 10:23-33). Further, that this was not the binding of part of the Mosaical code upon all Christians, in all areas, at all times, is evident by the fact that Paul said it was alright to eat meat sacrificed to idols if it offended no one (See past references). (b) First Sabbatarians say all the old law of Moses was abolished except for the Decalogue, then they begin to add even the law of Moses. They're just like the Jews (Acts 15:1,5)! If this is the binding of part of the old ceremonial law, then that in Acts 21:20-26 is also binding. Yet Sabbatarians do not go into Jewish temples and perform the rite of purification. Why not? If one is binding so is the other. If not, why not? Of course, any honest student of the word can see these things were done primarily for expedience sake and not to bind the old law upon Christians.

2. That which is to be included in a covenant is only that which is specifically included in it and not all of another covenant which is not specifically abrogated (See I Corinthians 9:21).

Acts 16:13 "And on the sabbath day we went forth without the gate by a river side, where we supposed there was a place of prayer; and we sat down, and spake unto the women that were come together."

ASSERTION: This shows Christians assembled on the sabbath day for Christian worship—"prayer"—even when not in the synagogue amongst Jews.

ANSWER: This text says nothing whatsoever about Christians assembling or worshipping. This deals with a Jewish place of worship, a Jewish worship service and a Jewish day of worship.

1. This was a Jewish place of prayer (cf Syriac and Greek). Philippi was a Roman colony (V.12) and evidently did not have a synagogue. Thus the Jews and proselytes—"worshippers of God" (V.14;8:27; See 13:14)—had designated places of prayer (Ibid.10:2,9,30). Paul

"supposed" the river side to be such a place (either due to its ideal location or through inquiry). Yet this says nothing at all about this being a place where Christians assembled for worship. This only shows Paul going there to teach and not to worship. This is merely another example of his taking advantage of circumstances to teach people and not to assemble with Christians to worship.

2. Those assembled were not Christians. Neither Lydia nor her household had yet obeyed the gospel. She did not become a Christian until after she and those with her had already assembled (V.15). Thus this was a place where non-Christians assembled and not Christians! (She and her house were likely Jewish proselytes.)

Acts 17:2-See Acts 13:14

Acts 18:4-11 "And he (Paul) reasoned in the synagogue every sabbath, and persuaded Jews and Greeks... V.11 And he dwelt there a year and six months, teaching the word of God among them."

ASSERTION: Paul kept over seventy sabbaths in a row. Thus how can anyone say it isn't necessary for Christians to keep?

ANSWER; Paul could have kept a thousand sabbaths in a row and such would not make it mandatory for Christians to keep, anymore than his circumcising a thousand like Timothy would make circumcision mandatory (Acts 16:3; Galatians 2:3ff), or his keeping of hundreds of other Jewish customs would make them mandatory (Acts 20:16; 21:20-26; I Corinthians 9:20). Also, notice the following:

1. Paul was not meeting with Christians when he assembled on the sabbath in this text; he was meeting with **Jews** and **Greeks** (proselytes) in the **synagogue**, persuading (V.4 - "sought to persuade" is literal) them to accept Christ. Thus, since they were not yet Christians, then this is not an example of a Christian assembly at all (See Acts 13:14).

2. Paul did not assemble on the sabbath for over seventy weeks—"year and six months"—in a row. He left the Jews when they rejected Christ and turned to the Gentiles after only a few sabbaths (V.5ff). Pure Gentiles did not keep the sabbath! Consequently, neither did Paul assemble for over seventy sabbaths in a row.

Acts 20:7 "And upon the first day of the week, when we were gathered together to break bread, Paul discoursed with them, intending to depart on the morrow; and prolonged his speech until midnight."

ASSERTIONS

One: This was not the Lord's Supper (which would santify the day) but merely a common meal (Acts 2:46).

Two: These met, according to the Jewish method of reconing time (evening to evening), on Saturday evening and not Sunday (TEV;NEB). Notice Paul did not believe Sunday was the sabbath day, for he traveled 18 miles to Assos (V.13f) on the following morning, Sunday, which he would never have done if it were the sabbath.

ANSWERS

One: That this was the Lord's Supper and no common meal can be determined from the text itself.

1. Notice they were **assembled** for the breaking of bread. Now Christians partook of the Lord's Supper in their assemblies (Acts 2:42; cf I Corinthians 11:20-34 - concerning the abuse of the Supper). Thus this was no common meal! Notice Paul's breaking of bread in a common meal after midnight (V.11—"He" and not the assembly) was separate from the breaking of bread (Lord's Supper) in the assembly (V.7).

2. These had come together for the specific purpose of breaking bread ("were gathered together" is passive, meaning they were gathered by another's authority, by

divine command - Hebrews 10:25; I Corinthians 11:26- "do it often"). Of course, since this was the primary purpose of their assembling, they would have done so immediately (though not mentioned) and would not have waited until after midnight. Also, the entire assembly is not recorded as breaking bread in verse eleven. (Which also was not on the first day of the week!) Yet, if this breaking of bread was only a common meal and not the Lord's Supper (in verse seven), then why did Luke make it a point to mention the specific day, the first day? The early Christians ate common meals together in one another's homes quite frequently, often every day in the week (Acts 2:46). Thus what would make this daily common meal any more important than those partaken on the other days? (Paul and his party had been in Troas for a week - V.6) This was no common meal on a common day; this was the Lord's Supper on the Lord's Day (See I Corinthians 11:20; Revelation 1:10).

3. The early church fathers confirm that the early Christians assembled on the first day of the week to partake of the Lord's Supper. These historians even used the same term, "breaking bread", to denote such (See "The Teaching of the Apostles," Ch. 14; Justin Martyr, "First Apology," Ch. 67; See historians at Revelation 1:10).

Two: The assertion that this was "Saturday evening" is indeed inaccurate. Yet it is actually irrelevant. For Saturday evening, according to Jewish reckoning, would still be the first day of the week and not the seventh (which ended at sundown)! It was not likely Saturday evening for the following reasons:

1. Troas was a Roman colony and not a Jewish one. Troas was Rome's second capital in Asia and was considered a part of Italy, being exempt from the land tax (See F.F. Bruce, "The Book of Acts"). Thus they would

logically observe Roman time and not Jewish. (Roman days began at midnight.) Luke records Jewish time when dealing with Jews (Acts 2:15) and Roman time when dealing with Romans (Acts 23:23 - "Third hour of night" would be nine at night, as night was reckoned from six o'clock P.M.).

2. Paul wouldn't likely depart from the Christian fellowship on the first day of the week, the Lord's day. Thus it is better to place this assembly on Sunday evening rather than Saturday evening and his departure on Monday morning. Of course, the first day of the week is not a sabbath day. **All** sabbath days were abolished (Colossians 2:16). And Paul would not have violated any laws of the New Testament by traveling on the first day of the week if he would have left on it. Yet doesn't it seem ironic that Sabbatarians would conclude that Paul wouldn't travel so far (18 miles) on Sunday if it were the sabbath, and then they turn right around and travel over a 100 miles to assemble on the seventh-day sabbath?

3. The literal Greek doesn't say "Saturday evening." It says on the "first of the week" (or first of the seven). Again and again, Sabbatarians choose translations which are lacking in accuracy and which they think support their teachings.

GOOD POINT: Notice that Paul's companions were in Troas through several sabbaths (Acts 20:5), and yet they are not recorded as assembling on any of them. Rather they are recorded as assembling on the first day of the week! Why?

Acts 21:20-26 - See Acts 15:19-21; cf 13:14.

Acts 25:8 "While Paul said in his defence, Neither against the law of the Jews, nor against the temple, nor against Caesar, have I sinned at all."

ASSERTION: Paul did nothing against the ten commandment

law of the Jews; so he must have kept the sabbath.

ANSWER: This does not refer to the ten commandment law of the Jews but to the entire old law of the Jews. Only Sabbatarians see the words "ten commandment" in this text. Also, I didn't know Sabbatarians believed the ten commandments were laws of only the Jews! Paul used this same line of defense earlier before Felix and appealed to his honoring the ceremonial aspects of the law and not the ten commandments (Acts 24:10-21, see V.18 "purified"). Thus, according to Sabbatarians, Christians must keep all the law of the Jews, doing nothing against it. Why don't they? Naturally, Paul, a Jew, did nothing contrary to Jewish law and custom while in the presence of Jews (unless it was bound as law upon Christians for justification - Acts 15:1-5; Galatians 2:3-5), for to the Jews he became a Jew (I Corinthians 9:20). Yet this does not mean he kept the sabbath as a part of the New Testament law. And, if you will look carefully, you will see there is absolutely no mention of the sabbath anywhere in this entire context!

1. Also, notice Paul did nothing contrary to the "temple" of the Jews. Does such mean we should honor the Jewish temple as God's holy habitation? Absolutely not (I Corinthians 3:16; Ephesians 2:21f).

2. Further notice that Paul did nothing contrary to "Caesar." Does such mean we must look up the old Roman law and keep it also? Absurd!

Acts 28:17—Seek Acts 25:8

ROMANS

Romans 3:19 "Now we know that what things soever the law saith, it speaketh to them that are under the law; that every mouth may be stopped, and all the world may be brought under the judgment of God."

ASSERTION: This says all the world – "every mouth . . . all the world" —is under the ten commandment law and not just the Jews.

ANSWER: This neither mentions the ten commandments as being "the law" nor teaches that all the world was/is under the law.

1. The law under discussion is the entire Old Testament law which was given only to the Jews (Romans 2:17-26; 3:1f; 9:4; cf Deuteronomy 4:8; 5:1-3; Psalm 147:19f; Amos 3:2; Malachi 4:4). There is no mention of the so-called separate "ten commandment law" here (See Deuteronomy 31:24-26). To say this law is just the ten commandment law is pure assumption. (Paul just finished quoting from Psalms and Isaiah and not the Decalogue- V.10-18). Thus Sabbatarians would seek to bring Christians under the judgment of the entire old law, which law Paul said even the Jews, much less the Greeks, were no longer under (Romans 6:14f).

2. The entire world was never directly under any of the Old Testament law. Paul had just mentioned how the Gentiles were "without the law" (the entire Old Testament law, including the Decalogue) and under their natural law, i.e., the moral law of their conscience (Romans 2:12-15; cf I Corinthians 9:21; Galatians 2:14ff; 4:21ff). Sabbatarians would have Paul contradicting himself in the same discourse! Yet the Gentiles, being without God's written law, were still convicted as sinners, for they could not **do** what they naturally thought was right and good—their conscience accusing them (Romans 2:15; 3:9; cf 14:23). But what about the Jews? Were they any less sinners than the Gentiles because they had God's written law to guide them? They should have been but were not. For everyone of those **under** the law (meaning the Jews only, or Paul would not have needed to make the distinction)—"every mouth"—was

silenced because they all had broken God's written law. It condemned every responsible Jew as a sinner (Ibid. 3:9,23). Even the Gentiles recognized this sin in Israel (Ibid. 2:24). Yet, if God's peculiar people were found to be sinners, then how much more were the Gentiles sinners who walked without such divine guidance. Thus the Jews, under the law, served as a showcase in the world as to how sinful all men—"all world"—were. (The Gentile being condemned in his conscience by the same moral transgressions as he saw the Jew being condemned for by his law.)

Now, it must be understood that this text tells us the purpose of the old law before the cross, during the Jewish dispensation, and not now (Galatians 3:19-25). "**Now**" a new system, the New Testament law of faith and liberty (Romans 3:27; James 1:25), bringing a righteousness "apart from the law," is in force (Romans 3:21). As the Gentiles looked to the Jew and his law and realized how sinful he was (as was also the Jew), so now all men can look at Christ's perfect example of righteousness, his sacrifice and new covenant and see how sinful they are. (Actually, men still understand they are sinful even if they have never heard of Christ or his new covenant. Their conscience still accuses them. Also, the laws that be further this conviction.) Thank God for righteousness "apart from the law" which said "thou shalt not" and if you do you "will die" (Ibid. 3:21; 7:7-9; 8:2)! **Note:** The Old Testament law is still the same as it was when Paul wrote this letter to the Romans. When men read it today, they will still primarily find nothing but a witness to man's sinfulness and not salvation. God forbid that some one or group would bring anyone to it as a Savior!

Romans 3:31 "Do we then make the law of none effect throught faith? God forbid: nay, we establish the law."

ASSERTION: The new law of faith (New Testament) did not abolish the ten commandment law; it rather established it!

ANSWER: Paul is discussing the principle of law here, and neither the Old nor the New Testament law is being specifically established.

1. There is no mention of the "ten commandments" in this verse or the entire chapter. It is blind assumption that reads such here.

2. There is no article "the" before the word "law" in this verse. Thus it is not referring to the Old Testament law or any other law specifically. It is the principle of law that is established through the law of faith. Paul had just pointed out the inability to save of both the Gentiles' natural law and the Jews' written law (Romans 3:9; cf 3:19). No law can save within itself (Ibid. 3:20; Galatians 2:16). Consequently, some might accuse Paul of being against all law (antinomian, as Sabbatarians accuse so many of being). This accusation had to be stopped before it started. Thus Paul simply affirmed that the law of faith (justification on the basis of faith in Christ and not by one's law-works) did not give license to do evil and set aside all law—moral, religious and civil (Romans 6:1f; 13:1ff). Rather, the law of faith established the purpose of all law. Law has one primary purpose—to point out one's crimes and sins. (Breaking of law is sin - I John 3:4). Yet, without a Saviour and another system of salvation, then all laws seem arbitrary and without purpose as far as man's eternal well-being is concerned. For, if one breaks one law, he is as much a lawbreaker as if he had broken all laws (James 2:10). Thus, once a person sins once, he may as well keep on sinning and breaking law (if not by grace forgiven and declared just), for what's to be gained by further law-keeping? Keeping a thousand laws

perfectly after becoming a transgressor will not erase the fact that one is still a transgressor and lost. Thus law alone is self defeating. But Christ's law of faith gives purpose to all law. For those who understand they are accounted as righteous on the basis of faith, which includes walking in the light and confessing sins (I John 1:7-9), have an incentive to live the best they can (Ibid. 3:1-3).

Romans 4:15 - See Romans 5:12-14

Romans 5:12-14 "Therefore, as through one man sin entered into the world, and death through sin; and so death passed unto all men, for that all sinned: for until the law sin was in the world; but sin is not imputed when there is no law. Nevertheless death reigned from Adam until Moses, even over them that had not sinned after the likeness of Adam's transgression, who is a figure of him that was to come."

ASSERTION: Man has always been under the ten commandment law, for without it there would be no sin (cf also Romans 4:15). That the ten commandment law existed from Adam to Moses is confirmed by the existence of death since Adam, which death is resultant of sin or breaking the law.

ANSWER: It is utterly false that sin could not be in the world without the ten commandments.

1. The ten commandments are not mentioned in this text or in chapter four, verse 15. Such is erroneously assumed. To say one cannot sin without breaking the ten commandments is entirely untrue (See comments at Genesis 2:2f - Four 2).

2. The ten commandments, as a codified system of law, did not exist from Adam to Moses. Paul even indicates

here that there was a different law system in effect from "Adam to Moses," meaning from Adam until the law (cf Galatians 3:17-19). The Bible teaches the ten commandments were given with the rest of the old law through Moses and not Adam (Deuteronomy 5:1-15; cf II Corinthians 3:6ff; John 1:17; 7:19).

Romans 6:14 "For sin shall not have dominion over you: for ye are not under law, but under grace."

ASSERTION: This means we are no longer under the curse of the ten commandment law and not that we are not under its authority, else we could commit wickedness without breaking the law.

ANSWER: There is no mention of the "ten commandments" in this text. If any specific law is being discussed as no longer over us, then it is the entire Old Testament law, being contrasted with the system of grace which took its place (John 1:17). Thus, if we are under its authority, as they contend, then we are under the authority of the entire old law, thus fallen from grace (Galatians 5:3f). Such is false! Likely, since there is no definite article before the word "law," Paul is dealing with law in general. We cannot be condemned by any law just because we fail to keep all its demands perfectly, for God, through his grace, forgives our failures and justifies us. Thus the Sabbatarian hasn't a point to argue in this text. Let's further refute his erroneous interpretations concerning this verse.

1. The phrase "under law" means under the authority of the law and not just under the curse of the law. This can be seen by the use of this same phrase in other passages. (a) I Corinthians 9:20—Was Paul under the curse of the Jewish law? No! Yet, by his own volition, he submitted to many of the things the law required or authorized (when expedient and not demanded). (b) I Corinthians 9:21—Was Paul under the curse of the law

of Christ? No! Paul was under its authority. The primary purpose of Christ's law, as it relates to Christians, is to save and not condemn (cf Romans 8:1ff). (c) Galatians 4:4—Was Christ born under the curse of the law? Was he born totally depraved? No! (No one is!) In fact, Christ never was subject to the curse of the law, for he never violated it in a single point (Galatians 3:10). His death, a curse in our behalf, was because of the sins of men and not sins of his own (Galatians 3:13). But Christ was born when the old law was still in authority—under the law (cf Luke 2:21-24). (d) Galatians 4:21—Did the Galatians desire to be under the curse or the authority of the law? Obviously, the authority (Ibid. 5:3). Thus, if the law here (Romans 6:14) being discussed is the ten commandment law, then we are not under its authority! (Indeed the law includes the ten commandments.)

2. Just because we are not under the Old Testament law does not mean we can work wickedness without breaking law or sinning. Christians are under the law of Christ (I Corinthians 9:21). Such is a law of liberty, though, and not a law designed to bring us into bondage all over again (James 1:25; Galatians 5:1ff). Also, just because we are not under any law for justification purposes (not even the keeping of the laws of the New Testament will bring justification on the basis of merit) does not mean we are free to sin (Romans 6:1f,15; Galatians 5:13). Indeed, God forbid! Yet, under the law of Christ, we first live—by grace through faith—then do them, being just opposite of the Old Testament law and all other laws which say "do and live" (Romans 10:5; Galatians 3:12). **Note:** This does not mean one is saved before completely obeying the gospel, including being baptized, which is an act of faith (Galatians 3:26f; See this writer's book "There Has Always Been One Baptism," Ch.4).

Romans 7:1-6 - See Romans 7:12,22 - One. 2.

Romans 7:12,22 "So that the law is holy, and the com-

> mandment holy, and righteous, and good ...V.22 For I delight in the law of God after the inward man."

ASSERTIONS

One: The ten commandment law—the law which says "Thou shalt not covet" (Exodus 20:17)—is holy and good. Therefore, such a law was not and could not be abolished.

Two: Paul here (V.22) said the ten commandment law of God was his delight. This was over twenty years after it was supposedly abolished!

ANSWERS

One: This, as usual, does not say the "ten commandment law" is holy and good (though they were); this says "the law" is holy and good. We have seen so many times already that the term "the law" cannot be limited to just the Decalogue. Yet the ten commandments, being the basis of the law, are many times referred to as the Mosaical law (See Deuteronomy 31:24-26; cf Genesis 26:5 on the word "commandment"). Thus just because Paul alluded to one of the ten commandments ("covet") does not mean he was confining his point about the holiness of the law to just the Decalogue, for they are found in the Mosaical law, the Pentateuch, and this one on coveting is even in the so-called ceremonial section of the Mosaical law (cf Deuteronomy 7:25). Also, all of God's laws, not just ten of them, are holy and good (Nehemiah 9:13; Psalms 119: 128,160,172). Even the ceremonial law of Moses was holy and good, being replete with holy objects (altars, candlesticks, showbread, garments, etc.), holy places (Hebrews 9:2f), holy observances and holy days (day of atonement, Passover, etc.). Perhaps the Sabbatarian would like to point out one law in the Old Testament which was not holy, right and good. He knows better. Yet even Sabbatarians admit that all the Old Testament, save the Decalogue and a few ordinances, was abolished—all those holy, right and good laws! Thus just because something is holy and good does not mean it cannot be abolished. Let's notice a few more things about this law Paul said was holy and good.

1. This law, as holy and good as it was, had only the power to condemn and kill and not to save and give life (Romans 7:9-11; cf II Corinthians 3:7).

2. This holy law is the one we were discharged from (Romans 7:6). This Old Testament law, including that which contained the law against coveting, the Decalogue, has no authority over the Christian for two reasons: (a) The law is dead to the Christian (Romans 7:2f). Notice the husband represents the law and the woman those under it. It is the husband (law) who dies. Dead men have no control over their former wives (cf I Corinthians 7:39). The law is dead to me, having been nailed to the cross (Colossians 2:14).[2] (b) The Christian is dead to the law (Romans 7:4-6). The old law system has as much control over me as the U.S. Constitution has over those buried in Arlington Cemetery. None! I died to the law when I was buried with Christ in baptism (Ibid. 6:3ff). **Note:** Please keep in mind that when we speak of the old law system being abolished, of which the Decalogue was the basis, that we speak in reference to the entire old covenant as a binding covenant upon us today. Christians keep nine of the ten commandments because they are morally right (the sabbath was not a moral principle - See Exodus 20:8-11 - Two.2) and thus included in the new covenant (cf Romans 13:9 on coveting; See I Corinthians 9:21); but he does not keep them because he believes the old covenant is still in force. It isn't!

Two: Paul's delighting in the "law of God" (V.22) does

---

2. Perhaps this first section (Romans 7:1-3) is merely illustrative of the premise that death frees both parties and is not here dealing with the death of the law. Other passages can be cited which do tell of its demise (Colossians 2:14ff).

not mean he believed the ten commandment covenant was still binding. First of all, the seventh chapter of Romans could very well be speaking of Paul's life before he became a Christian—of Paul as a Jew. If one compares chapter seven with chapters six and eight, he will see a great difference between the two Pauls: one indwelt by sin and nothing good (7:17); the other indwelt by righteousness and the Spirit (6:12f, 16-19; 8:4-13). Surely Paul delighted in all the Old Testament law before he became a Christian (Galatians 1:14). Secondly, Paul's expressing his general attitude towards **all** of God's laws (it does not say the "ten commandment law of God"), even if speaking from a Christian viewpoint, does not mean he was under the Old Testament law and the Decalogue covenant, for he already made it clear that he wasn't (Romans 6:14; 7:6; cf 8:2). Paul recognized the New Testament as God's superior law which superseded the entire Old Testament law. This was the one and only law he was under and a minister of (I Corinthians 9:21; II Corinthians 3:6ff)!

Romans 10:4 - Christ is the **end** of the law (cf Romans 3:31; 8:3f; See also Matthew 5:17-19; Galatians 3:19ff).

Romans 14:5 "One man esteemeth one day above another: another esteemeth every day alike. Let each man be fully assured in his own mind." (cf Romans 14:23)

GOOD POINT: Paul here clearly shows that no day, the sabbath included, can be exalted as inherently better than another (cf Galatians 4:10; Colossians 2:16). Even the first day of the week is not more holy than any other day. It is true that many great and holy things happened on the first day of the week (Revelation 1:10), and it is also true that Christians have been commanded to assemble, give and partake of the Lord's Supper (in general to worship) on the first day, but he is also to live a holy life of worship every other day (Acts 2:46; Romans 12:1). Thus, though the first day is special to the Christian, it is not "sacramentally" superior.

FIRST CORINTHIANS

I Corinthians 7:19 "Circumcision is nothing, and uncircumcision is nothing; but the keeping of the commandments of God (is something-GNW)."

ASSERTION: Paul said the important thing in Christianity is to keep the ten commandments.

ANSWER: As usual, the Sabbatarian assumes the word "ten" to be before the word "commandments." And as usual, it is not! The word "commandments" cannot be limited to the ten commandments in the Old Testament much less the New (See Genesis 26:5 - 1-2; Genesis 2:2f - Four.2; Ecclesiastes 12:13 - One). Paul understood the "commandments" to be that which had been revealed by Christ and his apostles in the New Testament (I Corinthians 7:10; 9:21; 14:37; II Thessalonians 3:4,6,10,12). If Sabbatarians would keep the commandments of the New Testament, they would not seek to bind the ten commandments as a covenant nor the sabbath as a command (II Corinthians 3:6ff; Colossians 2:16).

I Corinthians 9:21 "To them that are without law, as without law, not being without law to God, but under law to Christ, that I might gain them that are without law."

GOOD POINT: The Christian is only under the authority of the law of Christ (cf Galatians 6:2). This law contains the Lord's words as first spoken by him unto his apostles while in the flesh and then delivered unto us by them (Acts 1:2; Hebrews 2:3f; I Thessalonians 4:2; II Peter 3:2; Jude 3,17; cf John 13:20; 14:26; 16:13; 17:20). This law, commonly referred to as the New Testament/Covenant, was ratified as the only law for Christians at Calvary (Hebrews 9:15-17; cf 13:20). This is the "perfect law of liberty"

(James 1:25; Galatians 5:1; Romans 12:2; and see Galatians 4: 21--31), the "law of faith" (Romans 3:27; Jude 3), the "law of the Spirit of life" (Romans 8:2; cf II Corinthians 3:6f) and the "gospel" (Philippians 1:27). The Christian is not under the Old Testament law, including the Decalogue, which was mediated through Moses. He is solely under the covenant of grace and truth as mediated through Christ (John 1:17; I Timothy 2:5 cf Galatians 1:6-9; See comments at II Timothy 2:15).

What is binding in Christ's new covenant? Only that which is specifically included is binding. It does not include, in addition to what is specifically stated, everything from the Old Testament which was not specifically abrogated. Normal covenants include only that which they specifically outline and not also everything from previous or related covenants not specifically deleted. By way of illustration: An American citizen must only keep the laws recorded in the American law system. He does not need to seek out all the civil laws which were present in the previous British law system, from which many of America's laws were adopted, and keep all of them which were not included (nor specifically abrogated) in the American system. It is true that many of the American laws are identical to the British laws, but Americans keep them because they are a part of the American system and not because they were/are a part of the British. In like manner, just because Christians keep many laws under the New Testament which were formerly kept by the Jews under the Old Testament does not mean they are keeping them because of Old Testament authority, anymore than does an American keep British law when he keeps a law parallel to a law in it. Any law a Christian keeps he keeps because of New Testament authority, and New Testament authority alone.

Now is the sabbath command included in the New Testament? Is it authorized? No! It is neither commanded, regulated nor exemplified as to be kept by Christians. Every conceivable sin is mentioned in the New Testament but not the sin of violating the sabbath, a common sin in the Old Testament: twenty-one sins are mentioned in Romans 1:29-31, yet not the sin of violating the sabbath; ten sins in I Corinthians 6:9f, yet not concerning the sabbath; fifteen sins in Galatians 5:19-21, yet not concerning the sabbath; ten (±) SINS IN Ephesians 4:25-31, none concerning the sabbath; six sins in Ephesians 5:3f, none concerning the sabbath; eleven sins in Colossians 3:5-9, no sabbath; seven sins in I Timothy 1:9f, no sabbath; eighteen sins in II Timothy 3:2-4, no sabbath; eight sins in Revelation 21:8, no sabbath; (cf Mark 7:21f). Why this absence concerning the sin of violating the sabbath? If the sin of breaking the sabbath was to be the supreme sin (according to Sabbatarians), marking all violators with the mark of the beast (See Revelation 14:11f), then why wasn't it ever mentioned, predicted or warned against? Also, every moral commandment — idolatry (which covers the first two commandments of the ten), killing, adultery, swearing, coveting, bearing false witness, honoring parents, and stealing—are included many times in the teachings of the Lord's apostles, but not the sabbath command (Romans 2:21f; 7:7; 13:9; Ephesians 6:2; James 2:11; 5:12; cf Matthew 5:21ff; 19:18f). Again I ask, why the absence? The only mention of sin concerning the sabbath is in reference to some who were unlawfully binding it (Colossians 2:16; cf Galatians 4:10; Romans 14:5). The only command concerning it is that telling Christians not to allow anyone to bind it upon them (Colossians 2:16)! Yet, even if there were no passages such as these against enforcing the keeping of sabbath, Christians would still not be under obligation to keep it, for they are not specifically commanded to do so! Thus the request of Sabbatarians for one New Testament passage proving the sabbath was abolished does not actually have to be fulfilled (especially since they don't accept such when given such), for the silence of the New Testament concerning Christians having to keep it is sufficient as proof of abolishment. (Most Old Testament practices were not specifically abolished, things like the Passover, Pentecost, the Jubilee, incense, instrument of music in worship etc. Yet the silence of the New Testament concerning the necessity of keeping such abrogates such.) But, on the other hand, the Sabbatarian is under obligation to present **one passage** from the New Testament authorizing sabbath-keeping for Christians. This he cannot do! It is not required by the New Testament! It is not in the New Covenant!

I Corinthians 16:2 "Upon the first day of the week let each one of you lay by him in store, as he may prosper, that no collections be made when I come."

ASSERTION: This was just a normal business transaction which was put off from Friday until Sunday because the shops (which Christians ran) closed late on Friday, and they had to immediately keep the sabbath. Thus, since they couldn't work or take care of such business matters on the sabbath, they would logically do so after the sabbath and at home.

ANSWER: Since when is giving money for the Lord's work just a businss function? The very purpose for which this money was being set aside refutes such an absurd idea and sanctified the giving of it. Giving isn't work; it's worship (Deuteronomy 16:16f; Philippians 4:18). Notice some other erroneous assumptions and conclusions about the Sabbatarian's assertion:

1. **Such is to assume that all** the Christians in Corinth and Galatia were shop-keepers. Surely they didn't **all** own their own private businesses! This is not to mention the assumption that they all kept the sabbath—which isn't even mentioned in the text!

2. Where did Sabbatarians get the idea that it was wrong

to count or lay aside money on the sabbath? The Lord said it was good to do good on the sabbath (Matthew 12:10-12). Yet Sabbatarians now want to tell us that one couldn't set aside money for the Lord's work—in this case feeding those **starving** in Jerusalem—on the sabbath. Such is every bit as absurd as some of the arbitrary regulations made up by the Pharisees concerning the sabbath. Also, if it was unlawful then to take care of such money-matters on the Sabbath, then it would be unlawful now. If such be so, then why do Sabbatarians unlawfully take up collections on the sabbath?

3. Why don't Sabbatarians lay money aside at home on the first day of the week rather than collecting it in their assemblies on the sabbath?

4. If this was just a normal business transaction, then couldn't Christians just as easily have laid the money aside on Monday, Tuesday, etc.? Why did Paul see the need to specify the exact day? Maybe some of them didn't get paid on Friday! Isn't the real reason for this specific instruction the fact that they normally assembled on the first day of the week? And when better to take up such collections than when all the saints came together? If they did not collect this in the assembly (did it at home as Sabbatarians assert but don't practice), then would not such make the commanding of a specific day without purpose? Also, would not such actually create the very problem Paul was seeking to avoid? That of having to go to each Christian's home to collect it—"no collections when I come" ? By the way, common treasuries did exist then (John 12:6; Acts 4:35; 6:1).

5. The church historians confirm that collections were taken up on the first day of the week and in the assembly (Justin Martyr, "First Apology," Ch. 67). I wonder where they got the idea or the authority to do so?

SECOND CORINTHIANS

II Corinthians 3:6-18 "V.6 Who also made us (apostles) sufficient as ministers of a new covenant; not of the letter, but of the spirit: for the letter killeth, but the spirit giveth life. V.7 But if the ministration of death, written, and engraven on stones, came with glory, so that the children of Israel could not look stedfastly upon the face of Moses for the glory of his face; which glory was passing away: V.8 how shall not rather the ministration of the spirit be with glory? V.9 For if the ministration of condemnation hath glory, much rather doth the ministration of righteousness exceed in glory. V.10 For verily that which hath been made glorious hath not been made glorious in this respect, by reason of the glory that surpasseth. V.11 For if that which passeth away was with (or through) glory, much more that which remaineth is in glory. V.12 Having therefore such a hope, we use great boldness of speech, V.13 and are not as Moses, who put a veil upon his face, that the children of Israel should not look stedfastly on the end of that which was passing away: V.14 but their minds were hardened: for until this very day at the reading of the old covenant the same veil remaineth, it not being revealed to them that it is done away in Christ. V.15 But unto this day, whensoever Moses is read, a veil lieth upon their heart. V.16 But whensoever it shall turn to

> the Lord, the veil is taken away. V.17 Now the Lord is the Spirit: and where the Spirit of the Lord is, there is liberty. V.18 But we all, with unveiled face beholding as in a mirror the glory of the Lord, are transformed unto the same image from glory to glory, even as from the Lord the Spirit."

Note: Several arguments, often conflicting amongst themselves, have been set forth by Sabbatarians in attempting to rob this text of its obvious meaning—that the Decalogue was done away.

ASSERTIONS

One: That recorded on stones (V.7) was not the Decalogue but that recorded by Joshua when Israel crossed the Jordan (Deuteronomy 27:2f; Joshua 8:32).

Two: That which was passing away was only the glory in Moses' face and not the Decalogue (V.7).

Three: That which passed away was only the death penalty of the Decalogue and not the Decalogue itself (V.7,9; cf Romans 6:14).

ANSWERS

One: Paul was not talking about that written on stones by **Joshua at Jordan** when Israel crossed over but that brought down by **Moses at Sinai** when God's glory shone in his face (V.7; Exodus 34:29ff).

Two: It is true that the glory of Moses' face was passing away (V.7), but it is not true that Paul's point in this chapter was that the glory in Moses' face passed away.

1. What would be Paul's point in proving that only the glory in Moses' face passed away? Such was quite obvious, even to the Jews, since Moses had been dead for over a thousand years by then. Moses wasn't continuing,

much less the glory in his face! (Actually, the glory in his face began to fade even while he was delivering the Decalogue to Israel - V.13.) Thus Paul's point was the significance of this passing glory, with what it signified. First, this passing glory in Moses' face was symbolic of the temporary nature of the law he was mediating. The law was to last only till Christ (V.14; Galatians 3:19). The law was an "**old covenant**" (outdated) when Paul spoke here (V.14; See Hebrews 8:13). Yet the Jews, due to their hardheartedness, were as blind to this temporary nature of the law as were those in Moses' day who were veiled from seeing the actual fading of its glory (V.13-16). Thus the passing and temporal glory respecting the old law is not to be compared with the abiding glory of the new and eternal covenant of Christ (V.11; Hebrews 13:20). Second, the inferior glory of the Decalogue was token of its inferior nature as contrasted with the new covenant. The old covenant could only give death, for the letter of the law, regardless of what type of material it is written on (stone, steel or paper), can only kill (V.6; Galatians 3:10). The Decalogue could only minister death also, for "thou shalt nots" could never give life (V.7; Romans 7:7-10). Thus how could such a covenant be as glorious as that which gives life and liberty, Christ's new covenant (V.6,17)? The old covenant was indeed gloriously mediated through a man, Moses (V.7,14f; cf John 1:17; Acts 7:37f; Galatians 3:19); yet the new covenant was personally delivered through the Son of God, in whom dwelled the very glory of God (V.18; 4:6; John 1:14; 17:5; Hebrews 1:2). Which is the more glorious? That which came with some temporal glory of God reflecting in a man's face or that which came directly from the Lord of glory (I Corinthians 2:8)?

2. Also, Paul did not end his discourse at verse seven; he continued and pointed out how more than just the

glory in Moses' face passed away, for that which the glory attended also passed away (V.11). Paul said "that" which came "with" (or through) glory passed away. The ministration of death written on stones, **the ten commandment covenant**, is **"that"** which came **"with"** glory. **It** came "with" the glory on Moses' face (V.7). **It** had—"hath"—glory(V.9).**It** was "made glorious" (V.10). (The glory certainly wasn't made glorious!) Further, Paul said this ministration of death was the "old covenant" (V.14) or the law of "Moses" (V.15) which passed away in Christ. ("Moses" is here used metonymically for the "law of Moses" - cf Acts 8:30; 13:39.) That this "old covenant" is the Decalogue is seen by the fact that the "veil" is used throughout this chapter in connection with the Decalogue (V. 7,13,15). "Moses" is also used in connection with the giving of the Decalogue, he being the minister of it (V.7). This old covenant is that which was done away in Christ, having been replaced with the new covenant (V.6,14; Hebrews 8:13; 9:1-4; 10:9). This again proves the passing away of the glory was not all Paul had under consideration. For the glory in Moses' face did not last until Christ came; it passed away at Sinai. Now Paul said that those who read this old covenant, meaning as a binding one, are blind to the true covenant of Christ and, having placed a veil upon their hearts, are as blind to the passing away of the old covenant as were the Jews to the fading of its glory at Sinai. (Such people cannot be expected to know the true Lord's day is not the sabbath!) Yet, for those who will turn to the Lord and his spiritual law, as revealed in the new covenant, the veil is removed and they realize the old law and its glory were both done away (V. 12-16).

Three: The "ministration of death" which passed away was not just the death penalty, being abolished because of the forgiveness of Christ. First, the word "death" does not grammatically agree with the word "engraven" but rather with the word "ministration." The ministration, being that which Moses ministered—the Decalogue, is that which was engraven on stones and is that which brought death. Nary a sinner was made alive by keeping the ten commandments. It condemned them all to death (Romans 3:9; 7:7ff)! (They were therefore saved by faith even in Old Testament times—Habakkuk 2:4). Second, the death penalty was not engraven on the tablets of stone at all. Only the law which brought death (Decalogue) was!

GALATIANS

Galatians 3:19 "What then is the law? It was added because of transgressions, till the seed should come to whom the promise hath been made. ."

ASSERTION: The law which was added was the ceremonial law of Moses to the moral law, the ten commandment law. Thus the only law abolished when the seed came was the ceremonial law of Moses.

ANSWER: The law which was added was the entire law of Moses, including the Decalogue, and it was not added **to** the Decalogue.

1. This verse does not say the "ceremonial law" was added. How assumptuous can one get? How inconsistent and contradictory can one be? The Sabbatarian freely adds the words "ten commandment" before the word "law" when it suits him, and now he wants to add the word "ceremonial" before the same word! He insists in one place that the term "the law" means only the moral law of the Decalogue and in another that it means just the ceremonial law of Moses. One could become quite confused in trying to figure out what the Sabbatarian really believes! Of course, this "law" is the same as the "book of the law" in verse ten, which book included all the laws written in the first five books of Moses, the Pentateuch. The ten com-

mandments are just laws and were recorded in the book of the law (See Deuteronomy 31:24-26 - Two; cf Nehemiah 8:1ff). (Note: If they were not recorded in the book of the law, then we would have no copy of them, for the tables of stone do not now exist!) Therefore, the law which included the Decalogue wasn't always in existence. According to this passage in Galatians, it was added 430 years after the covenant with Abraham and some 2500 years after Adam's creation (who, according to Sabbatarians, was supposed to have kept the ten commandments). Also, the Decalogue was not meant to continue as a covenant forever. It was to last until Christ—"the seed"—would come, fulfill it and replace it with the new law of faith (Galatians 3:19, 23-25; cf Matthew 5:17-19). **Note:** Some Sabbatarians say the law which was added was the ten commandment law as a formal covenant. They then maintain that it was not abolished when Christ came. They say only the penalty of the Decalogue was abolished and the ten commandments themselves were established as a law (Romans 3:31). Yet those who hold to such a position are few, for they are hard pressed to maintain any kind of consistency within their own doctrine. For to admit such is to admit that the ten commandment law was not always in existence (thus Adam was not under it as a formal covenant and, consequently, didn't keep the sabbath) and that it didn't continue past Christ (V. 19,23-25; See Matthew 5:17-19; Romans 3:31; 6:14 for their erroneous teachings on the words "till, established, under law").

2. This does not say any law was added to another, especially to the Decalogue. That covenant which Paul first presented as being in existence 430 years prior to the adding of the law was not the Decalogue covenant but the covenant of promise (V.8,16f). Now a covenant of promise is contrary to any covenant of law,

and law cannot be added **to** it (V.15-18). This does not say the law was added **to** anything; it says the law **was added**, meaning it was added along side the covenant of promise as a temporary measure until the seed (Christ) should come to whom the promise was made. The covenant of promise offered many blessings to man—forgiveness of sins, sonship with God, God's Spirit within (Acts 3:26; Galatians 3:14, 26-29; 4:6)—whereas the law was added only to point out their sins—"added because of transgressions"—and consequent need for the **promised** blessings of Messiah. Thus the law and the Decalogue had nothing in common with the covenant of promise nor with the new covenant which is the fulfillment of God's covenant of promise. The Christian cannot enjoy the promised blessings just by keeping the ten commandments (Galatians 4:21-31). He can only receive forgiveness of sins, sonship and the Spirit by following Christ's law of faith (Ibid. 3:26-29). Notice this law of faith contains a prerequisite, baptism, unto receiving these blessings (V.27). This requirement, incidently, is nowhere to be found in the ten commandments (cf also Acts 2:38)!

Galatians 4:10 "Ye observe days, and months, and seasons, and years."

COMMENT: Notice this covers all the Jewish holy days in chronological order.

"Days" - weekly days of observance, like **sabbath days!**

"Months" - monthly observances, like new moons.

"Seasons" - seasonal observances, like the yearly feasts, Pentecost, etc.

"Years" - sabbatical years, like the Jubilee (See Colossians 2:14-17).

Galatians 4:21-31 "V. 21 Tell me, ye that desire to be

under the law, do ye not hear the law? V.22 For it is written, that Abraham had two sons, one by the handmaid, and one by the freewoman. V.23 Howbeit the son by the handmaid is born after the flesh; but the son by the freewoman is born through promise. V.24 Which things contain an allegory: for these women are two covenants; one from mount Sinai, bearing children unto bondage, which is Hagar. V.25 Now this Hagar is mount Sinai in Arabia, and answereth to the Jerusalem that now is: for she is in bondage with her children. V.26 But the Jerusalem that is above is free, which is our mother. V.27 For it is written, Rejoice, thou barren that bearest not; Break forth and cry, thou that travailest not: For more are the children of the desolate than of her that hath the husband. V.28 Now we, brethren, as Isaac was, are children of promise. V.29 But as then he that was born after the flesh persecuted him that was born after the Spirit, so also it is now. V.30 Howbeit what saith the scripture? Cast out the handmaid and her son: for the son of the handmaid shall not inherit with the son of the freewoman. V.31 Wherefore, brethren, we are not children of a handmaid, but of the free woman."

GOOD POINTS

One: Paul knew nothing of the making of two covenants—one moral (Decalogue) and one ceremonial (law of Moses)—at Sinai. He said only **"one"** came from Sinai (V.24). Now wasn't the Decalogue given at Sinai? Yes, it was (Galatians 3:19; II Corinthians 3:6ff)! Then it is the one under consideration here, or Paul should have made sure that no one would confuse the ceremonial covenant given at Sinai (asserted) with the moral covenant also given there! He didn't, though, because only one covenant was given there. And that covenant is the one we are no longer under (V.21); that is the covenant of flesh and not promise (V.23,28f); that is the covenant of bondage and not freedom (V.24f); and that is the covenant which Christians are to cast out (V.30)! (Notice that "Hagar" stands for the Sinaitic covenant and "her children" for the Jews who trust in the works of the law.)

Two: The new covenant did not have its origin at Sinai but from the heavenly Jerusalem (which is "above"), or the church (V.26; cf Hebrews 12:22; Micah 4:2). Thus Christians are not under bondage to the Sinaitic covenant, including the Decalogue, which **then** had its headquarters in physical Jerusalem ("now is" V.25) and **now** in churches of the Sabbatarian persuasion! No, Christians do not put their emphasis on the ark of the covenant that was in the physical temple in physical Jerusalem but on the new covenant which is the spiritual Jerusalem, the church (cf Jeremiah 3:16).

EPHESIANS

Ephesians 2:15 "Having abolished in his flesh the emnity, even the law of commandments contain-in ordinances. . . ."

ASSERTION: Only the laws contained in "ordinances" were abolished, i.e., the ceremonial laws of Moses and not the moral laws of the Decalogue.

ANSWER: "Ordinances" are not just ceremonial rules and regulations. They also pertain to moral commands of God. Fornication is an ordinance (cf Acts 15:29 with 16:4), and surely fornication is moral. (It is actually the same physical act as adultery - I Corinthians 5:1.) An ordinance is defined as an authoritative decree or direction, order, law or command (Vine; Webster). The ten commandments were all decrees, saying, "thou shalt not." The ten commandments were called ordinances (Deuteronomy 5:1ff; Hebrews 9:1-4). Thus the law contained in ordinances, being the first covenant, was taken away (Hebrews 9:1-4; 10:9). **Note:** It should be pointed out that even if the "ordinances" could be confined to just the ceremonial aspects of the law (which we have seen they cannot be) that the Decalogue would still be abolished with them, for the moral and ceremonial made up only one covenant. And, since the greater and most burdensome part of the old law was ceremonial in nature, then it would naturally be mentioned as the greater cause of the abolishment of the entire law. Yet the entire old law died with the death of the ceremonial; just as an entire person dies when his circulatorial system is defective, even though his mind may be good (cf Romans 7:1-6).

PHILIPPIANS

N/A

COLOSSIANS

Colossians 2:14-17 "V. 14 Having blotted out the bond written in ordinances that was against us, which was contrary to us: and he hath taken it out of the way, nailing it to the cross; V.15 having despoiled the principalities and the powers, he made a show of them openly, triumphing over them in it. V.16 Let no man therefore judge you in meat, or in drink, or in respect of a feast day or a new moon or a sabbath day: V.17 which are a shadow of the things to come; but the body is Christ's."

ASSERTIONS

One: The law which was nailed to the cross (V.14) was not the ten commandment law but that contained in "ordinances" (ceremonial laws) which was "against us" (the ten commandments are not against us).

Two: The sabbath mentioned as abolished in this text (V.16) is not the seventh-day sabbath (weekly) but the ceremonial sabbaths (monthly, yearly). You will notice that it does not say the "weekly sabbath day" was abolished. Such is erroneously read into the text! You will also notice that the word "sabbath" is plural in the Greek— "sabbaths." This definitely proves Paul was referring to the ceremonial **sabbaths** and not the weekly **sabbath**. Further, you will notice that the sabbaths under consideration were those which were "shadows" of things to come (V.17). The weekly sabbath was/is a memorial of something in the past, the creation, and not a type of something future. Thus the only sabbaths Paul is discussing are those ceremonial, typical sabbaths and not the weekly sabbath.

ANSWERS

One: The ten commandments were "ordinances" (See Ephesians 2:15). They were also "against us." They were against all who could not keep them perfectly, for there was no "forgiveness clause" contained within them! They only brought **death** to man (Romans 7:7-10; II Corinthians 3:7,9). Now I'd say that was against us! Also, the breaking of the sabbath brought death to more than a few (Exodus 31:15; Numbers 15:32ff), and I'd say that was contrary to us! Thus the ten commandments perfectly fit the description of that presented here. Thank God Jesus nailed it, along with its curse, to the cross! Thank God for Christ's new covenant which is **for** us, bringing forgiveness to us (Hebrews 8:12).

Two: That the sabbath in this text is the weekly sabbath is obvious inspite of the fact that the word "weekly" does not precede it. All the facts mentioned in this text force one to this conclusion and no other. Thus the inference that it is the "weekly sabbath" is a fair inference and not an erroneous assumption. Yet, before going into these facts, I must point out the unfair and inconsistent reasoning of the Sabbatarian in accusing anyone of making unjust inferences or erroneously reading into the text. For how can the Sabbatarian say it is wrong to infer the word "weekly" into the text on the grounds that Paul did not specifically say "weekly sabbath," and then turn right around and read an entire theory and line of words into the same text? Granted, the word "weekly" is not in the text and has to be inferred. Yet, tell me, do the words "ceremonial, yearly, monthly" appear in the text before the word sabbath? They certainly do not! The Sabbatarian read them into the text. And, I might add, that the Sabbatarian's inference is unwarranted in light of that which is revealed in the text. Let's look further at their assumptions and assertions.

1. The Sabbatarian's argument that the word "sabbath" is plural in this text does not prove it is not the weekly sabbath. It, as a matter of fact, helps in proving such! For the word used here is the same root word used throughout the Bible in reference to the weekly sabbath. It is the Greek word "sabbaton" (genitive plural). It can be translated either singular or plural. (For "sabbaton" see Exodus 20:8; 35:3; Leviticus 23:38; 24:8; Numbers 15:32; 28:9; Deuteronomy 5:12; Isaiah 58:13; Matthew 12:2; 20:1; Luke 4:10; Acts 13:14; 10:13; for other plural forms referring to the weekly sabbath see "sabbasi" and "sabbata" Exodus 20:10; 31:13; Isaiah 56:2, 4; 58:13; Ezekiel 20:12; Matthew 12:5, 10,12; Luke 4: 31; Acts 17:2; etc.) Now this word sabbaton, or one of its forms, is used some sixty times in the New Testa-

ment alone, and Sabbatarians understand it to be referring to the **weekly** sabbath in every instance but this one! Yet Paul made it very clear that he was still referring to the weekly sabbath, for he used the same word and form (sabbaton—genitive plural) here as was used in the very giving of the sabbath command: "Remember the sabbath day" (sabbaton-genitive plural, Exodus 20: 8 - LXX)! Only a blind person could fail to see this is the weekly sabbath. Now the Sabbatarian leaders know **this** plural word is used for the weekly sabbath throughout the Bible, and the very use of such an argument shows how deceitful they really are!

There are yet other reasons why this is the weekly sabbath. (a) In the New Testament the Jewish feasts and holy days, other than the weekly sabbath, are not spoken of as sabbaths. Thus to do so here is unwarranted. Also, it might be of some merit to note that in the Greek/Septuagint Version of the Old Testament, wherein the specific word Sabbaton occurs, that only one feast day – the annual Day of Attonement – is referred to using the word Sabbaton (Leviticus 23:32). And, in that regard, it would appear rather confusing to insist upon referring to that which occurred only once a year as the "sabbaths" (plural) and yet to that which occurred fifty-two times a year as the "sabbath" (singular)! Actually, the annual D.O.A. falls into Paul's second category, the "feast days," and not the "sabbaths" (Numbers 29:7ff, 39). And thus the word "sabbaths" here is practically limited to being understood to be only the weekly sabbaths!

(b)

Paul's list of abolished days is synonymous with the Old Testament lists of Jewish observances which included the weekly sabbath as given here (See Numbers 28:9). Notice how the sabbath in this list is the **weekly** sabbath: "meat and drink"—the **daily** rituals; "feast days"—the **yearly** or seasonal days; "new moon"—the **monthly**; "sabbath" —the **weekly**! The progression is daily, yearly, monthly and what is left—the **weekly**! The first three observances in this list cover all the Jewish holy days but the weekly sabbath. It is therefore the only one left to be understood by the term "sabbaths!" If the weekly sabbath was not what Paul had in mind, then he would certainly be guilty of causing the greatest confusion (I Corinthians 14:33). **Note:** It is a scriptural fact that the weekly sabbaths were actually **ceremonial** observances. They headed the list of all such ceremonial observances (Leviticus 23:2ff). Something which is ceremonial is something which is external in form and observance (Webster). Now the sabbath was such an external observance. One could see if he or another was resting on the seventh day. Thus, if all ceremonial sabbaths were abolished, as even Sabbatarians admit, then so was the weekly sabbath abolished, for it was ceremonial! (It was not a moral law - See Exodus 20:8-11 - Two.2.)

2. The argument that the weekly sabbath was a memorial and not a type or shadow is also inaccurate. First of all, the sabbath was not so much a memorial of the creation, to be observed by all men, as it was a reminder to the Jews of their deliverance from Egyptian bondage (Deuteronomy 5:15). It is true that the seventh day was chosen by God because he rested on it, but it was not given by him just to commemorate **his** resting. It was rather given to Israel that they might commemorate **their** resting from the serfdom of Egypt. Also, that which is a memorial of something past can be a shadow or type of something future. The Passover was a memorial of deliverance from Egypt (Exodus 12:11-14); yet it was also a type of Christ's sacrifice for our sins (I Corinthians 5:7). In like manner, the sabbath also foreshadowed the greater, spiritual rest to be enjoyed by the disciples of Christ in time and eternity (Matthew 11:28; Hebrews 4:1-11). Thus the sabbath was among those shadows fulfilled in Christ. And, when the spiritual antitype became a reality, the physical type passed away! I might

add, that, since Paul said the sabbath was such a type or shadow, that it does not matter who wants to argue that it's not—it still is! **Note:** The argument that the word "which" (V.17) only modifies the word "sabbath" (V.16), meaning only those sabbaths which were shadows were abolished, is grammatically incorrect. "Which" is nominative and "sabbaths" is genitive. Thus the word "which" modifies the entire list. They were all shadows, including all sabbaths!

FIRST THESSALONIANS

N/A

SECOND THESSALONIANS

N/A

FIRST TIMOTHY

I Timothy 1:8 "But we know that the law is good, if a man use it lawfully."

ASSERTION: The ten commandment law is good and has a purpose—by helping man to live righteously (V.9ff)—in the salvation of man.

ANSWER: As usual, this does not say the "ten commanment law" is good but "the law" (V.8 - the entire Old Testament law) or "law" (V.9 - law in general). That Paul was not alluding to just the Decalogue is proven by his inclusion of laws not found in the Decalogue: "abusers of themselves with men, men stealers, liars, any other thing contrary to the sound doctrine, according to the gospel" (V.9-11). Notice Paul didn't say the law he was speaking of was good to be used to correct or punish "sabbath breakers!" Let's notice a few more things about the proper use of law:

1. The law is good only if used "lawfully." Now the Old Testament, including even the ceremonial aspects,

shadows, historical events, etc., has a lawful purpose for Christians. It can be used for our historical learning, for examples, for teaching and for study about the nature of God, the creation, moral precepts, justice, etc. (cf Romans 15:4; I Corinthians 10:11; II Timothy 3:16). Yet this has nothing to do with binding the Old Testament as the Christian's authority and guide in redemption (one cannot be saved by faithfully conforming to the requirements of the old law), worship (its sacrifices are now unlawful), government of the church (the kingdom is no longer a national one, as was Israel), etc. If the Sabbatarian intends to bind the law on the basis of this text, then he must bind the entire Old Testament law, because such is the meaning of the term "the law" (See Deuteronomy 31:24-26 - Two). This he maynot do, for Paul made it clear that that which is to be bound must be according to the "sound doctrine" and "gospel" (I Timothy 1:10f) . Thus the Christian is only bound by that bound in the law of Christ (I Corinthians 9:21; See II Timothy 2:15). The Sabbatarian, by indiscriminately binding the laws of the Old Testament, uses the law unlawfully!

2. The law, as mentioned in this context, is not for the righteous but the unrighteous (V.9). Only unrighteous folk need a list of "thou shalt nots" to keep them in line. In fact, as soon as a person asks for a law prohibiting him from doing something which is obviously contrary to what love for God and man would naturally dictate, then he shows his unrighteous nature. The righteous live by higher ideals than mere restraining codes (Matthew 22:37-40; Romans 13:9b-10). They serve God and live righteously out of "newness of spirit" (having been recreated - John 3:5; Acts 2:38) and not "oldness of letter" (Romans 7:6; II Corinthians 3:6; Hebrews 8:10). Thus the laws, as here given, are for the purpose of showing the sinner (heathen) how sinful he is and

how much he needs the Saviour. Yet these laws, in and of themselves, cannot save man nor make him perfect in righteousness. Only Christ and his law of faith can accomplish such (Philippians 3:9; cf II Corinthians 5:21)!

SECOND TIMOTHY

II Timothy 2:15 "Give diligence to present thyself approved unto God, a workman that needeth not tc be ashamed, handling aright (rightly dividing - KJV) the word of truth."

GOOD POINT: This matter of "handling aright . . . rightly dividing the word of truth" is the crux of the matter in all problems arising over the binding of Old Testament practices, observances and days. Those who fail to distinguish between the Old and New Testaments, equally binding both, are ever in conflict in their teaching. And, until they recognize the New Testament as the sole authority for Christians, they will ever remain in conflict and contradiction (See I Corinthians 9:21). The binding of the sabbath is a classic example of not rightly dividing between the Testaments. Those who teach it is still binding are constantly found fleeing to the Old Testament (or to the Gospels where men lived under its authority—Galatians 4:4; Hebrews 9:15-17) for their proof texts. They must do this, for there is no New Testament authority for keeping it, only abolishing it! Yet isn't it ironic, that, while Sabbatarians do not recognize this lawful division between the Testaments, they do continuously divide, in both the Old and New Testaments, between the so-called moral and ceremonial laws, between "the law" and "law," between "the law of God" and "the law of Moses," between that which was inside the ark and that outside the ark, etc? These divisions are nowhere authorized in the Bible, and they are contradictory, illogical and unscriptural!

II Timothy 3:15f "And that from a babe thou (Timothy) hast known the sacred writings which are able to make thee wise unto salvation through faith which is in Christ Jesus. Every scripture inspired of God (is inspired of God - cf KJV) is also profitable for teaching (doctrine - KJV), for reproof, for correction, for instruction which is in righteousness...."

ASSERTION: The "sacred writings" and "scriptures" are without a doubt the writings of the Old Testament (especially the ten commandments), for the New Testament did not exist when Timothy was a babe. Thus the Old Testament scriptures bring salvation and are profitable for doctrine.

ANSWER: The "sacred writings" would indeed be the Old Testament writings, **all of them** and not just the ten commandments! "Every scripture" would include every verse in the Old Testament and not just a few Sabbatarian-selections! They were all inspired, were they not? or was just the Decalogue God's word? Now do Sabbatarians mean we are under the entire Old Testament, including all the ceremonial laws as well? Must we keep it all to be saved and have the correct doctrine? If so, then why do they fail to recognize as essential about 99% of the "sacred writings" and "inspired scriptures" as contained in the so-called ceremonial law? (Remember that the ceremonial made up the bulk of the old law!) Also, "every scripture" would include the New Testament scriptures, for they are all inspired of God. (Much of the New Testament had already been written at the time of this writing.) Why don't Sabbatarians heed those New Testament scriptures which say the Old Testament scriptures are no longer binding (Acts 15:1-11; Romans 6:14; 7:1-6; II Corinthians 3:14; Galatians 3:19-25; 5:1-4; Hebrews 8:13; etc.)? There is more:

1. The "sacred writings" (Old Testament scriptures) are indeed capable of making one wise **unto** salvation (towards salvation), pointing him to salvation by faith in Christ (V.15b; Galatians 3:24f; cf Acts 8:32-35 for a case in point), but they contain no sacrifice which can remove sin and no instructions whereby one might be saved through the sacrifice of Christ! Let any one find the instructions of how to be saved by the blood of Christ in the Old Testament. Only the New Testament tells men how to enter his death (symbolically speaking) and be washed from sins in his blood (Acts 2:38; 22:16; Romans 6:3ff) Thus the Old Testament, though it brings no salvation, points man to the salvation of Christ as revealed in the New Testament. He who has read the Old Testament is wise enough to know this!

2. The word translated "doctrine" (KJV) is better rendered "teaching" (ASV), for the Greek word, didaskalia, is better understood in the active sense—"the teaching" than in the passive, the thing taught—"doctrine" (Vine). Surely, all the Bible can be used for teaching purposes (cf I Timothy 1:8); yet it can't all be bound upon Christians as required "doctrine." (Must we build an ark as did Noah?). Of course, Paul is including the New Testament, God's full and final revelation, in these "inspired scriptures." The Old and New Testaments are both profitable. They complement one another as long as one "rightly divides the word of truth" (cf II Timothy 2:15).

TITUS

N/A

PHILEMON

N/A

HEBREWS

Hebrews 1:1f; 2:2-4 "God, having of old time spoken unto the fathers in the prophets by divers portions and in divers manners, hath at the end of these days spoken unto us in his Son... For if the word spoken through angels proved stedfast, and every transgression and disobedience received a just recompense of reward; how shall we escape, if we neglect so great a salvation? which having at the first been spoken through the Lord, was confirmed unto us by them that heard; God also bearing witness with them, both by signs and wonders, and by manifold powers, and by gifts of the Holy Spirit according to his own will."

COMMENT: The old covenant, that spoken by God through the prophets and angels (of Galatians 3:19), spoken of throughout the book of Hebrews refers to the entire Old Testament. The new covenant spoken of throughout this book, though promised in the Old Testament (Jeremiah 31:31; cf Galatians 3:6), does not refer to anything spoken prior to the incarnation of Christ. It contains that which was finally spoken through God's Son – "first spoken through the Lord" – and then delivered with confirming power through his holy apostles – "them that heard" (2:4; See 7:12, 18f-22; 8:6–13; 9:1–4,15–20; 10:9; 12:24; 13:20; for the changing of the law).

Hebrews 3: 11, 18- See 4: 1-11

Hebrews 4:1–11 "Let us fear therefore, lest haply, a promise being left of entering into his rest, anyone of you should seem to have come short of it. V.2 For indeed we have had good tidings preached unto us, even as also they; but the word of hearing did not profit them, because it was not united by faith with them that heard. V.3 For we who have

> believed do enter into that rest; even as he hath said, As I sware in my wrath, They shall not enter into my rest: although the works were finished from the foundation of the world. V.4 For he hath said somewhere of the seventh day on this wise, And God rested on the seventh day from all his works; V.5 and in this place again, They shall not enter into my rest. V.6 Seeing therefore it remaineth that some should enter thereinto, and they to whom the good tidings were before preached failed to enter in because of disobedience, V.7 he again defineth a certain day, Today, saying in David so long a time afterward (even as hath been said before), Today if ye shall hear his voice, Harden not your hearts. V.8 For if Joshua had given them rest, he would not have spoken afterward of another day. V.9 There remaineth therefore a sabbath rest for the people of God. V.10 For he that is entered into his rest hath himself also rested from his works, as God did from his. V.11 Let us therefore give diligence to enter into that rest, that no man fall after the same example of disobedience."

ASSERTION: A keeping of sabbath, the seventh-day sabbath (V.4), remains for God's people (V.9).

ANSWER: This does not say a "keeping of sabbath" remains for God's people; this says a "sabbath rest" remains, i.e., a rest like unto God's rest on the seventh day after creation. It is an abiding rest that remains and not a keeping of a religious ordinance. Such a notion is totally contrary to the writer's entire point in chapters three and four, that the rest which Christ has to offer is so much greater that that which Moses offered (3:3). Yet, if all Christ has to offer is the keeping of the same old sabbath the Jews had been keeping since Moses, then wherein is his rest better? That this isn't the keeping of the seventh-day sabbath is obvious from the text itself:

1. The "sabbath rest" (V.9) under discussion is not the keeping of the seventh-day sabbath on the earth, for even those who kept it were said not to have entered into this sabbath rest. Notice the Jews who fell in the wilderness, who had kept the sabbath day many years since their exodus from Egypt, did not enter into the rest under consideration here—God's rest (Hebrews 3:11, 16:19; 4:5f; cf Exodus 16:30)! Also, the Jews had been keeping the sabbath for centuries, after Joshua led them into Canaan (V.8), when David said they had not entered into this rest (V.7f)! Further, these Jewish Christians, to whom the writer addresses in this letter (to "Hebrews"), may have kept the seventh-day sabbath as a custom at the time of writing (according to some church historians), yet they still were told to "give diligence to enter" into the rest under consideration (V.11). Thus they had not yet entered into the sabbath rest mentioned in this chapter, specifically in verse nine. Now, if the rest of the seventh-day sabbath had been entered into by all of these without entering into the rest under consideration, then the rest spoken of for God's people to enter is not the rest of keeping the seventh-day sabbath! What then is this rest? (Next point)

2. The rest which remains to be entered into is God's rest. Notice it says it is God's rest – "my rest . . . his rest" (3:11; 4:1,3,5,10). God's ceasing from his labors on the seventh day after creation (4:3f) is therefore typical of the rest which awaits the Christian when he departs this earth and enters heaven's rest (4:10f; Revelation 14: 13). Meanwhile, the Christian has the spiritual rest in

Christ to give him comfort in this life (Matthew 11:28). And I might add that this spiritual rest is far more comforting, helping to ease the burdens of life much more, than the physical day of rest on the sabbath ever was!

Hebrews 7:18f "For there is a disannulling of a foregoing commandment because of its weakness and unprofitableness (for the law made nothing perfect)...."

ASSERTION: The law which was cancelled was that which "made nothing perfect," being the ceremonial law of Moses (V.12-14) and not the ten commandment law, which law is **perfect**, holy and good (Psalms 19:7; Romans 7:12).

ANSWER: This does not say the "ceremonial law" made nothing perfect; it says "the law" made nothing perfect. (Notice this has the definite article before the word law, and Sabbatarians usually contend that such refers to the ten commandment law!) This doesn't say the law was cancelled because it was imperfect; this says it was cancelled because it was weak, unprofitable and couldn't perfect. Now the entire Old Testament law system was perfect (See Psalms 19:7; Romans 7:12), yet it was weak in power to save, as weak as the weakest link—man (Romans 8:3; Hebrews 8:8). It was thus unprofitable for God's purposes, for he could not fulfill his desire to save man through it; and it was unprofitable for man, for he could not perfect his guilty conscience by keeping it (Hebrews 9:9, 14; 10:1-3). Yet this weakness of the law applied to the entire law and not just to the ceremonial aspects. The ten commandments could not fulfill God's purpose to save man either. No man was ever forgiven of sin by keeping the ten commandments. No man ever cleansed his guilty conscience by keeping the ten commandments. Thus the entire Old Testament law was perfect as a law system (let the Sabbatarian show imperfections in any of it as far as law is concerned), but it was not perfect as far as being a system of salvation. Man needed a covenant which could perfect him. Man needed a better covenant for imperfect men (Hebrews 7:22; 13:20f; cf Colossians 1:28). So God cancelled the old covenant — "the law which made nothing perfect" — and gave us the new and better covenant, the perfect law of liberty (See Hebrews 8:6ff; 9:1-4; 10:9; James 1:25).

Hebrews 8:6-13 "But now hath he obtained a ministry the more excellent, by so much as he is also the mediator of a better covenant, which hath been enacted upon better promises. V.7 for if that first covenant had been faultless, then would no place have been sought for a second. V.8 For finding fault with them, he saith, Behold, the days come, saith the Lord, That I will make a new covenant with the house of Israel and with the house of Judah; V.9 Not according to the covenant that I made with their fathers In the day that I took them by the hand to lead them forth out of the land of Egypt; For they continued not in my covenant, And I regarded them not, saith the Lord.

V.10 For this is the covenant that I will make with the house of Israel After those days, saith the Lord; I will put my laws into their mind, And on their heart also will I write them; And I will be to them a God, And they shall be to me a people: V.11 And they shall not teach every man his fellow-citizen, And every man his brother, saying, Know the Lord: For all shall know me, From the least to the greatest of them. V.12 For I will be merciful to their iniquities, And their sins will I remember no more. V.13 In that he saith, A new cove-

> nant, he hath made the first old. But that which is becoming old and waxeth aged is nigh unto vanishing away."

ASSERTION: The "first covenant" here spoken of is not the Decalogue covenant but the people's covenant (or "promise") to keep the Decalogue (Exodus 19:8). This first covenant was based on **human promises** to keep God's ten commandments (V.6); whereas the new covenant is based on **God's promises** to write his ten commandments on our hearts (V.10) and to forgive us when we fall short of perfection (V.12). These indeed are better promises (V.6). Also, the fault with the first covenant was not with the Decalogue (for it is holy and good) but with "them" (V.8), meaning with those who broke their promises to keep the ten commandments (V.9b).

ANSWER: The so-called, separate people's covenant does not exist (See Exodus 24:7f - One). Only one covenant sprang from Sinai, God's, and not two, the people's and God's (V.9; Galatians 4:21-31; cf Deuteronomy 29:1). This one covenant is that which God made with Israel and not they with him—"I made...my covenant" (V.9). (The people's agreement to keep God's covenant did not constitute a separate covenant.) This "first covenant" included the ten commandments (9:1-4 - "tables of stone") and was the only one ratified at Sinai (9:18-20; cf Exodus 24:7f).

1. Concerning the "better promises" (V.6). (a) Where does it say the promises upon which the first covenant was based were the people's promises to keep God's ten commandments? Such an idea isn't in the text!

The promises upon which the first covenant was founded were God's promises to make Israel a great nation and a people for his own possession, providing they kept his covenant (Exodus 19:5f). God also promised to curse them as a nation if they failed to keep it (Deuteronomy

27:26; cf chapters 28-30). Thus the first covenant was based upon God's promises and not the people's. Yet these promises were inferior to God's new covenant promises; the promise of forgiveness (Hebrews 8:12); the promise of Sonship (Ibid. 8:10b); the promise of the Spirit within (these first three promises fulfill God's promise to Abraham - Acts 3:26; Galatians 3:14,26-29); and the promise of heaven (Hebrews 4:9-11; 9:28; 11:10, 16). (b) Where does it say God established his new covenant on the promise to write the ten commandments on our hearts? Besides the fact that the promises are much more comprehensive than such (See point a), there is the obvious fact that this doesn't say God would write the "ten commandment laws" on our hearts! It just says "laws" (Ibid. 8:10)! Again Sabbatarians boldly assume what they have consistently failed to prove!

2. Where does this say the "fault" (8:8) of the first covenant was with the people's promise to keep the Decalogue? It doesn't! The fault was not with their promises; it was with **them**! They were sinful, faulty, and the first covenant could not perfect them (See Hebrews 7:18f; cf Romans 8:3).

3. Several important facts about the "first covenant" and the "new covenant" can be learned from this important chapter. (a) The new covenant is unlike — "not according to" — the first covenant which God made with "the fathers" after bringing them out of the land of "Egypt" (V.8f). The first covenant made with these fathers after Egypt definitely included the ten commandments (I Kings 8:9,21; Deuteronomy 5:1-15). Thus, since the new covenant is unlike this first covenant, then the new covenant is not the Decalogue — restated or revised! One very obvious difference of the new covenant from the first covenant is the absence of the sabbath command! (b) The new covenant superseded the first or old covenant (V.13). The law of Moses, including

the Decalogue, was an **old** (outdated) covenant, not just in the first century, but as this verse says — "In that he saith, a new covenant, he hath made the first old"— it was old when God spoke these words through Jeremiah some six centuries earlier! It, like all old things, became progressively older and feeble — "waxeth aged"— as time passed, and it, like all old and aged things, died — "vanishing away." It was near death in Jeremiah's day, for it was **old** — so declared by God himself! It died with our Lord on the tree (Colossians 2:14). Who wants to return to a dead old man (cf Romans 7:1ff)?

Hebrews 9:1-4 "Now even the first covenant had ordinances of divine service, and its sanctuary, a sanctuary of this world. V.2 For there was a tabernacle prepared, the first, wherein were the candlestick, and the table, and the show bread; which is called the Holy Place. V.3 And after the second veil, the tabernacle which is called the Holy of holies; V.4 having a golden altar of incense, and the ark of the covenant overlaid round about with gold, wherein was a golden pot holding the manna, and Aaron's rod that budded, and the tables of the covenant."

GOOD POINT: Notice that the "first covenant" (V.1) is the same as the ten commandment covenant—"tables of the covenant" (V.4). Only one covenant is mentioned in this text! Notice that this first covenant had "ordinances" (V.1). Thus two separate covenants—one ceremonial (ordinances) and one moral (ten commandments)—do not exist. Both ceremonial and moral laws are found in the same covenant, the "first covenant," which was done away (10:9).

Hebrews 9:9f- See Ecclesiastes 12:13

Hebrews 9:15-17 "And for this cause he is the mediator of a new covenant, that a death having taken place for the redemption of the transgressions that were under the first covenant, they that have been called may receive the promise of eternal inheritance. For where a testament is, there must of necessity be the death of him that made it. For a testament (or covenant) is of force where there hath been a death: for it doth never avail while he that made it liveth."

ASSERTION: Nothing added by the apostles after Christ's death can be considered a part of the new covenant, for once a covenant has been ratified no one can add to it (Galatians 3:15). This would be demanded if we maintained that nothing before Christ's death (ten commandments) is to be considered a part of the New Covenant. Since the former is not true, then neither is the latter.

ANSWER: The apostles did not add to Christ's covenant, as people like Ellen G. White and Joseph Smith have done; they, inspired by Christ's Spirit, only fully revealed it (John 14:26; 16:13; Hebrews 2:3f; cf Matthew 28:18-20). The new covenant is not the apostle's covenant; it is all Christ's! Thus only that bound by Christ through his New Testament apostles and prophets is binding and not that mediated through Moses or the Old Testament prophets (See I Corinthians 9:21).

GOOD POINT: A good point to bring out in this context is that the "first covenant" was not binding as a formal covenant until after it was ratified with blood by Moses (V.18ff; Exodus 24:7f). Therefore, the ten commandments, as a codified list and written covenant, were not kept by Adam, Abraham, etc., for the first covenant, including the Decalogue, was not then in force. Sabbatarians seek to escape this delimma by saying only the ceremonial covenant (of Moses - V.19f) is under consideration here. Yet, if such is so, then there is no record of the ratification of the Decalogue in the entire Old Testament. Thus they cannot prove anyone was legally obligated to keep the ten commandment covenant during the entire Old Testament period (V.15-17)! Also, if the ratification of the new covenant represents the ratification of the Decalogue, as some Sabbatarians assert (it isn't), then it still was not in force as a covenant until the cross. Such would still mean the Decalogue was not binding during the entire Old Testament period. (Of course, we know the Decalogue was ratified along with the rest of the first covenant in Exodus 24:7f.)

Hebrews 10:1 - Sabbatarians assert that the law under discussion here has nothing to do with the ten commandment law because it is the law which was a "shadow of things to come" (See Colossians 2:14-17 - Two.2).

Hebrews 10:9 "Then hath he said, Lo, I am come to do thy will. He taketh away the first, that he may establish the second."

GOOD POINT: The "first" covenant (8:7f,13; 9:18ff) contained the ten commandments (9:1-4) and was "taken away" (See II Corinthians 3:6ff)! One is only bound to keep the "second" covenant which was established at Calvary (9:15-17; See I Corinthians 9:21). One cannot keep both the old and new covenants (II Timothy 2:15; cf Galatians 5:1-4).

Hebrews 10:25 - See this writer's book "II Peter Three—Jewish Calamity or Universal Climax?" PP.54ff.

Hebrews 12:18-24 "For ye are not come unto a mount that might be touched, and that burned with a fire, and unto blackness, and darkness, and tempest, V.19 and the sound of a trumpet, and the voice of words (When God spoke the ten commandments—GNW); which voice they that heard entreated that no word more should be spoken unto them V.20 for they could not endure that which was enjoined, If even a beast touch the mountain, it shall be stoned; V.21 and so fearful was the appearance, that Moses said, I exceedingly fear and quake: V.22 but ye are come unto mount Zion, and unto the city of the living God, the heavenly Jerusalem, and to innumerable hosts of angels, V.23 to the general assembly and church of the firstborn who are enrolled in heaven, and to God the Judge of all, and to the spirits of just men made perfect, V.24 and to Jesus the mediator of a new covenant, to the blood of sprinkling that speaketh better than that of Abel."

GOOD POINT: The new covenant is not like the Sinaitic covenant (Hebrews 8:9). The new is based on things spiritual and the other on things that might be **touched** (V.18): things like the mount upon which the Sinaitic covenant was received; the ark in which it was contained: the stones on which it was written. The new covenant brings fellowship with God and the heavenly host; the old brought fear of God and separation (V.19-23). Thus Christians do not desire to bring into mind such physical and fearful things as associated with the giving of the ten commandment covenant at Sinai (cf Jeremiah 3:16). No, for Christ mediated a better covenant (V.24)!

Hebrews. 13:8 "Jesus Christ is the same yesterday and today, yea and forever."

ASSERTION: Since Jesus never changes (cf Malachi 3:6), then we must keep the sabbath as he kept it (Mark 1:21; Luke 4:16).

ANSWER: This does not say Christ never changes his law; this says **he** never changes, meaning his person. He is still God, still trustworthy, etc. That it cannot mean he never changes his law is obvious, for he changed his laws concerning the Passover, circumcision, sacrifices and, yea, his entire law (Hebrews 7:12; 8:6-13). He even changed the day of assembly and worship before he left this earth in the flesh, for he met with his disciples on the first day of the week and not on the seventh (John 20:19,26f)! **Note:** Other heretical teachers use this same verse to support their doctrines. For instance, those who teach that Christ is still working miracles today say he must for he never changes. Yet Christ is not still working miracles today, anymore than he is still providing manna from the sky to feed everyone! He can change his laws and methods of working. He has, for he now works through his new covenant to convince, convict and convert (John 20:30f). When we have his word we need no wonders!

Hebrews 13:20 - The blood of the eternal (new) covenant (cf 9:15-17; Matthew 26:28).

JAMES

James 1:25 "But he that looketh into the perfect law, the law of liberty, and so continueth,being not a hearer that forgetteth but a doer that worketh, this man shall be blessed in his doing."

ASSERTION: The perfect law is God's ten commandment law (Psalms 19:7; cf Romans 7:12). All who keep them shall be blessed.

ANSWER: This does not say God's perfect law is the "ten commandment law." Such is assumption. This says God's perfect law is the "law of liberty." Now that automatically eliminates the ten commandments, for they never liberated a soul from the bondage of sin. In fact, they only pointed out how terribly enslaved to sin man really was (Romans 7:7ff)! Thus the perfect (Gk. Teleion, meaning complete, mature) law of liberty is the complete gospel which frees man from the slavery of sin (John 8:32ff; Galatians 2:4; 5:1; cf Romans 12:2; I Corinthians 13:8-12; See Psalms 19:7).

James 2:8-12 "Howbeit if ye fulfill the royal law, according to the scripture, Thou shalt love thy neighbor as thyself, ye do well: V.9 but if ye have respect of persons, ye commit sin, being convicted by the law as transgressors. V.10 For whosoever shall keep the whole law, and yet stumble in one point, he is become guilty of all. V.11 For he that said, Do not commit adultery, said also, Do not kill. Now if thou dost not commit adultery, but killest, thou art become a transgressor of the law. V.12 So speak ye, and so do, as men that are to be judged by a law of liberty."

ASSERTIONS

One: The "royal law" (V.8) is the ten commandment law for part of it is quoted in verse 11, saying, "Do not commit adultery... Do not kill," the seventh and sixth commands.

Two: If we offend in one point, breaking one of the ten commandments (like the sabbath), then we are guilty of breaking all of them.

ANSWER:

One: The "royal law" is not the ten commandment law; it is the law which says "Thou shalt love thy neighbor as thyself" (V.8). Now James made this quite clear, but he did not mention the words "ten commandment!" In fact, this royal law, as quoted by James, isn't even found in the Decalogue. Rather, it is found in the so-called ceremonial law (cf Matthew 22:36-40). The laws quoted in verse 11 are found many times in the New Testament (cf Romans 13:9) and are thus binding upon Christians. Yet, as we have pointed out before, to allude to some of the laws which were in the Decalogue does not bind the entire Decalogue, anymore than James' alluding to the royal law, which was in the ceremonial law (V.8), makes all the ceremonial law binding (See I Corinthians 9:9,21: Matthew 19: 16-22, #3). Only that specifically mentioned as binding is binding. and you will notice that the sabbath is nowhere mentioned in this text!

Two: One becomes a transgressor of the old law James speaks of in 2:10 only if one brings himself under that law (Galatians 5:1–4). The Christian is under no such legal system of justification (Ibid. 2:16–21; Romans 6:14). And to assert otherwise is to trade grace for law, forfeit all hope and totally reverse the intent and teaching of this text. For James certainly was not trying to coach these Christians (mainly Jewish) to go back under such a legal system. Contrariwise, he was trying to caution them against bringing themselves under its jurisdiction by their: (1) Judaistic Actions – affording preferential treatment to their Jewish brethren, especially the rich, and that in spite of the fact that they persecuted Christians and blasphemed that name (V. 1–7)! Such conduct made them as one of them (Galatians 2:11ff). (2) Judaisitic Authority – appealing to the law of Moses (Leviticus 19:18) and their former, narrow interpretation of who their "neighbor" was (Jews) to justify their bigotry (V.8; of Luke 10:25–37).

All this, apart from repentance, would place them back under a law system that not only condemns such prejudice (V.9; Leviticus 19:15) but also indicts such sinners as transgressors of the whole law (V.10–11; Galatians 3:10–13; 5:3). Better to act as Christians should: judging all equally in need of a new law of liberty, grace, mercy and faith (V.12–13).

FIRST PETER

N/A

SECOND PETER

N/A

FIRST JOHN

I John 2:3-6 "And hereby we know that we know him, if we keep his commandments. V.4 He that saith, I know him, and keepeth not his commandments, is a liar, and the truth is not in him; V.5 but whoso keepeth his word, in him verily hath the love of God been perfected. Hereby we know that we are in him: V.6 he that saith he abideth in him ought himself also to walk even as he walked."

ASSERTIONS

One: Those who claim to know Christ but do not keep his ten commandments (sabbath included) are liars (V.3f).

Two: Those who would abide in Christ must walk as he walked. How did Christ walk? He kept all the ten commandments, including the sabbath command (Mark 6:2; Luke 4:16).

ANSWERS

One: This does not say "ten commandments." The Sabbatarian continues to assume what he has never been able to prove, that the word "commandments" means ten commandments (See Genesis 26:5). The commandments here alluded to by John are those given by Christ to and through his apostles (I John 2:7ff with John 13:34 - one which is not in the Decalogue; cf I John 3:23; II John 4; John 12:48).

Two: Christ, as pointed out before, was born under the Old Testament law and kept all of it (Galatians 4:4; See Mark 1:21). Must we keep the entire Old Testament law in order to walk in his steps? We must not! To abide in Christ we must abide in his doctrine, the New Testament (II John 9), and not in that which came through Moses, the Old Testament, which includes the Decalogue (John 1:17).

I John 3:4 "Every one that doeth sin doeth also lawlessness (transgresseth also the law - KJV); and sin is lawlessness (is transgression of the law - KJV)."

ASSERTION: Sin is transgression of the ten commandment law. Without the ten commandment law there would be no such thing as sin (Romans 4:15; 5:12-14).

ANSWER: Again the words "ten commandment" have been added by the Sabbatarian. Actually, this has no reference to any specific law — the Decalogue, entire Old Testament or New Testament. The ASV translates this more accurately, "sin is lawlessness," than does the KJV, "sin is the transgression of the law" (See also RSV, NASV, NEB, Greek Interlinear). Thus this refers to anyone who is wicked, lawless, sinful, and who oversteps all boundaries of what is morally right. An accurate translation removes their argument entirely! Also, we have already seen that one can sin without breaking the Decalogue, and especially can one sin without breaking it as a covenant (See Genesis 2:2f-Four. 2; Romans 5:12-14). John said all unrighteousness is sin (I John 5:17). This would include both sins of commission and omission (Romans 14:23; James 4:17; I John 3:17).

I John 3:22 "And whatsoever we ask we receive of him, because we keep his commandments and do the things that are pleasing in his sight."

ASSERTION: We must keep the ten commandments to have our prayers answered.

ANSWER: The same assumption as always, adding the word "ten" when not in the text (See 2:3-6). John, in the very next verse (V.23), shows he is not speaking of the ten commandments but the commandments to believe in the name of Jesus Christ and love one another. Neither of these can be found in the Decalogue (cf John 13:34).

SECOND JOHN

N/A

THIRD JOHN

N/A

JUDE

N/A

REVELATION

Revelation 1:10 "I was in the Spirit on the Lord's day..."

ASSERTIONS

One: The "Lord's day" is the day Christ is Lord of, the sabbath of the Lord (Exodus 20:10; Mark 2:28).

Two: The only authority for making Sunday the Lord's day is Rome (emperor or pope). This change was effected for the sake of the pagans who worshipped the sun — thus called "**Sun**-day." This was in fulfillment of prophecy (Daniel 7:25), and all who receive Sunday-keeping have the "mark of the beast" (Revelation 13:11-18; 14:11f).

ANSWERS

One: In answering the first assertion, I will first give reasons why the seventh day (Sabbath) is not the Lord's day, and then I will give reasons why the first day of the week is the Lord's Day.

Reasons why the seventh day (sabbath) is not the Lord's Day:

1. The seventh day, as far as Christ is concerned, points more to the defeat of a man than to the victory of the Lord. For on the seventh day, following his death, his body lay lifeless in the tomb. He had not yet been resurrected and declared Lord (Acts 2:36; Romans 1:4). Thus the only thing the disciples would remember in the keeping of the seventh day, if it were the day set aside for commemoration of the Lord, would be the defeat of their Lord (seemingly so at that time) and their despair and sadness (Luke 24:17-21). Such is not becoming of the Lord's day!

2. None of the foundation facts of Christianity — the resurrection of Christ, being the basis and hope of the gospel, the pouring out of the Holy Spirit, the beginning of the Lord's church, etc. — are relevant to the seventh day. Thus wherein is the seventh day a significant day for Christians? It was significant to the Jews because it was a token of their deliverance from Egyptian bondage (Deuteronomy 5:15). Yet there is no New Testament significance. So why keep it?

3. The seventh day was not the day especially set apart for Christians to observe any specific religious function. A day is a sanctified day only when certain religious observances have been specifically enjoined to be ful-

filled on it. Now the Jews had to rest and remember their deliverance from slavery on the sabbath. Yet we do not find Christians doing any special religious function specifically on the sabbath day. Thus, as far as Christians are concerned, the seventh day is not a special day sanctified unto the Lord — "the Lord's day." (All days, generally speaking, actually belong to the Lord - Romans 14:5-8.)

4. The seventh day, or the sabbath day, is never called the "Lord's day" in the Bible or in religious history. "Sabbath of the Lord" (Exodus 20:10) is not synonymous with "Lord's day" (Revelation 1:10), for the word "sabbath" is not found in the latter! Notice it does not say the "Lord's **sabbath** day" in Revelation 1:10! (Concerning Christ being the "Lord of the sabbath," see Mark 2:23-28 - Two.) The term "Lord's day" is a new term in the Bible, found only here in Revelation, and it would not be used to designate an old day. Now the seventh day had been known by the term "sabbath day" for over 1500 years when John wrote the book of Revelation, and he would not have confused matters by referring to it by an unknown appellative. He had always referred to the seventh day as the sabbath day and not the Lord's day in his gospel, so why would he change in this letter (John 5:9f,16,18;7:22f; 9:14,16; 19:31)? Especially since no one, neither the Jews nor Jewish Christians, called the seventh day anything else but the sabbath (See Acts 13:14,27,42-44; 16:13; 17:2;18:4)! They never referred to it as the "Lord's day." (Neither do Sabbatarians, except in debate!)

5. The New Testament says the sabbath was abolished (Colossians 2:16). Notice it was **abolished** and not **changed** to another day or another name! Consequently, the sabbath could not be the Lord's day.

6. The early church fathers, historians and writers say

the sabbath ceased to be the day religiously observed by God's people (See the testimonies of these in the confirmation of the first day as the Lord's day).

Reasons why the first day (Sunday) is the Lord's Day:

1. The first day of the week is rightly called the "Lord's day," because it was the day of victory for Christ and man. It was the day Christ was raised from the dead and declared with power to be God's Son and Lord over all (Matthew 28:1-6; Acts 2:36; 17:31; Romans 1:4; compare Psalms 2:7 with Acts 13:32f). Then, on this day which he made, he became the head of the corner (Psalms 118:22-24). It was on this day that he declared his lordship over all powers (Colossians 2:14f). It was on the first day of the week, later on Pentecost, when God's Spirit was poured out and bore visible testimony (by miracles) that Christ was sitting at God's right hand, confirmed to be Lord and Christ (Acts 2:33)[3] This was the day when man's redemption was completed (Romans 4:25) and his hope realized (I Peter 1:3). Thus the first day is a day of victory and joy for the Christian: "Oh Glorious Resurrection Day" (Luke 24:13-41; I Corinthians 15:54-57)!

2. All the great events of Christianity are related to the first day of the week. (a) The resurrection (Matthew 28:1-6). **Note:** Saturday was not the resurrection day (Mark 16:1f; Luke 24:1ff; See "Another Look at Seventh-day Adventism," Douty, p.81, footnote 58). (b) The gospel was first heralded forth on the first day, saying, "He is risen" (Matthew 28:6). This same message

---

3. "Pentecost," meaning "fiftieth," fell on the first day after the seventh sabbath, or on Sunday (Leviticus 23:15). It is true that some did not so reckon it, but those Jews—the Sadducees—who regulated the observance of Pentecost before AD70 did. Also, the Karaite Jews always held that Pentecost fell on Sunday. The ancient Syriac Bible says Sunday. The early church fathers concur (Philip Schaff, p. 63). Thus all the events recorded in Acts two, which occurred on Pentecost, can be assigned to the first day of the week, Sunday.

was later publically revealed for the first time on the first day of the week, on Pentecost (Acts 2:1-47; See footnote 3). (c) The Lord first appeared to his disciples on the first day of the week (Matthew 28:1, 8ff; Luke 24:13ff). (d) The Lord met with the assembly of the saints for the first two times on the first day of the week (John 20:19,26).[4] The disciples always assembled on the first day of the week thereafter (Acts 2:1; 20:7; I Corinthians 16:2). Even the Jewish Christians, though they kept the seventh-day sabbath as a custom for some years after Pentecost, kept the first day of the week as the day of Christian assembly and worship (See the testimonies of the church fathers in this section). (e) The Spirit was poured out to indwell every baptized believer on the first day (Acts 2:1, 17,33,38f). (f) The Lord's church was established on the first day (Acts 2:38-47). (g) The victory of the church was proclaimed on that day (Revelation 1:10). Now why did God choose to bring all these things to pass on the first day rather than the seventh day if not to sanctify it over the seventh day? It therefore does not matter what anyone wants to say about the first day of the week, it was truly the "Lord's day!"

3. All special or specific religious functions were observed on Sunday by the Christian church. (a) They assembled on the first day (See comments on Acts 20:7; I Corinthians 16:2; cf John 20:19,26). (b) They partook of the Lord's Supper on the first day (See Acts 20:7). (c) They contributed towards the Lord's work on the first day (I Corinthians 16:2). And, of course, they engaged in all the other acts of Christian worship on

---

4. The term "eighth day" (John 20:26) was the Jewish equivalent of the "first day." It certainly wasn't the "seventh day"! The church fathers used this same term in reference to the first day of the week on which the disciples assembled to worship (See "The Epistle of Barnabas," Ch. 15; Justin Martyr, "Dialogue with Trypho," Ch. 41; Cyprian, "Epistle 58," Section 4).

the first day, e.g., as singing, prayer and study of God's word (Acts 20:7; 2:42).

4. As we mentioned previously, the term "Lord's day" is a new term in the Bible, and it logically implies a new day. The Greek word used here for "Lord's" — Kuriake from Kuriakos — is only found one other time in the New Testament, in I Corinthians 11:20, speaking of the "Lord's Supper." This uniqueness is most significant, for we have the "**Lord's** Supper" (uniquely his) on the "**Lord's** Day" (also uniquely his). When better to have the Imperial Supper than on the Imperial Day? (We know the Supper was partaken on the "first day of the week" - Acts 20:7!) Everything about Christianity is new, and we should naturally expect the day Christians meet on to be new also (Psalms 118: 24). Christians are new creatures (II Corinthians 5:17); they have a new covenant (Hebrews 8:6-13); they have a new name — "Christians" and not "Jews" (cf Acts 11:26); they have a new feast—the "Lord's Supper" and not the "Passover" (I Corinthians 5:7; 11:20). When the Lord said he would make all things new, he did not intend to keep an old day, the sabbath. No, he replaced it with a new and better day—the Lord's day!"

5. The New Testament authorizes the first day of the week as the day when Christians are to assemble for worship (Acts 20:7; I Corinthians 11:20,25; 16:1f; Hebrews 10:25; Revelation 1:10). The first day of the week is not a sabbath of any kind, for it is never called such, and all sabbaths were abolished (Colossians 2:16).

6. The early church fathers confirm that the first day of the week was the "Lord's day," upon which Christians assembled to partake of the Lord's Supper, give of their means to support the Lord's work, sing, study and pray. (a) The Epistle of Ignatius to the Magnesians 9:1, (AD 107): "Those, then, who lived by ancient prac-

tices arrived at a new hope. **They ceased to keep the sabbath and lived by the Lord's day**, on which our life as well as theirs shone forth, thanks to him and his death'' (emphasis mine). (b) The Epistle of Barnabas, Ch.15, (AD120): ''Wherefore also we keep the eighth day with joyfulness, the day also on which Jesus rose from the dead.'' (c) The Teaching of the Apostles, Ch.14, (AD 125): ''But every Lord's day do ye gather yourselves together, and break bread....'' (d) Justin Martyr's First Apology, Ch.67, (AD 140-145): ''And on the day called Sunday, all who live in cities or in the country gather together in one place...(he then mentions the preaching, Lord's Supper, prayer, thanksgivings and givings which then took place)...But **Sunday is the day on which we hold our common assembly**, because it is the first day on which God, having wrought a change in the darkness and matter, made the world; and Jesus Christ, our Saviour, on the same day rose from the dead'' (emphasis mine). Justin Martyr, in his Dialogue with Trypho, also says that Christians did not keep the sabbath and that the first day was equivalent to the eighth day (cf Ch.41). (e) Dionysius, bishop of Corinth, cf Eusebius, Eccl. Hist. Bk.4, Ch.23, (AD170), said the Lord's day was a holy day. (f) Bardesanes of Edessa, Syria, (AD180), said the first day is a day of assembly. (g) Clement of Alexandria, Egypt Bk.7, Ch.12, (AD194), said to keep the Lord's day in glorifying the Lord's resurrection. (h) Tertullian of Africa, in his Answer to the Jews Ch.2; 4, (AD200), said the sabbath was not kept by Adam, Abel, Noah, Enoch and that the sabbath was only a temporary enactment. Also, in his Apology, Ch. 16, he said Sunday was to be kept instead of the sabbath. (i) Origen, Origen against Celsus, Bk.8, Ch.22, (AD225), said they kept the Lord's day. (j) The Apostolical Constitutions, Section 7, Para.59; Bk.7, Section 2, Para.30, (AD250), says they assembled on the Lord's day which was the resurrection day. (k) Cyprian, Epistle 58, Section 4, (AD 250), said the eighth day was the first day and the Lord's day. (l) Anatolius, bishop of Laodicea, Asia, seventh, tenth and sixteenth cannons, (AD 270), said they kept the Lord's Supper on the Lord's day which was the resurrection day. (m) Victorinus, bishop of Petau, Creation of the World, Section 4, (AD 300), said Christ abolished the sabbath. (n) Peter, bishop of Alexandria, Canon 15, (AD306), said the Lord's day is the day Christ arose. (o) Eusebius, bishop of Caesarea, the most noted and reliable of Biblical historians, Eccl. Hist., Bk.1, Ch.4, (AD 324), said that Christians did not observe sabbath and that even Judaizers kept Sunday as well as the sabbath. (p) Johann Von Mosheim, Eccl. Hist., Century I, Ch.IV, Para. 4; Century II, Part II, Ch.IV, Para. 8; Century III, Part II, Ch.IV, Para. 2; Century IV, Ch.IV, says the disciples met for centuries on the first day of the week and that even the Jewish brethren met on Sunday to worship. (q) Schaff-Herzog, Encyclopedia of Religious Knowledge, (AD 1891), says Sunday is the first day of the week and the day the church partook of the Lord's Supper. (See Canright, pp.218-233, for more information on all these historians.) Now all these historians, from all over the world (not just in Rome), covering history from a few years after the death of the last apostle of Christ, show Sunday was the day Christians assembled on, worshipped on and called the "Lord's day." This change from the sabbath took place without any religious wars or heated debates in the church due to outrage over the supposed defection. How was such a drastic change wrought without such if it was without Apostolic approval? How?

Two: The assertion that Rome (emperor or pope) is the only authority for keeping Sunday as the Lord's day has already been refuted in the first answer, having shown how it was kept by the Lord, his Apostles and the early Christians centuries before Constantine or the Catholic church ever existed! Also, such is contrary to the historical records concerning what the Catholic church actually claims and what the Roman Emperor, Constantine, did in regards to Christians observing Sunday (See comments at Daniel 7:25; Canright pp. 186-190, 210-214, 234-248).

1. The assertion that Sunday is merely a pagan day, due to the worship of the sun, has no force whatsoever. First, the Bible does not call the Lord's day Sunday; it calls it the Lord's day or the first day of the week. Second, just because the first day was called Sunday does not mean Christians worshipped the sun, anymore than the Jews (or Sabbatarians) worshipped saturn in meeting on "**Satur-**day" (saturn-day). All days of the week have been so named: Monday = moon-day; Tuesday = Tiw-day (god of war); Wednesday = Woden-day (chief god in German mythology); Thursday = thunder-day (god of the sky); Friday = Fria-day (goddess of love) (cf Webster's Dictionary).

2. Since the Lord changed the day of assembly and worship from Saturday to Sunday, then such a change could not be the fulfillment of the "change of the times" by any Roman king or pope as foretold by Daniel (See Daniel 7:25).

3. The assertion that "Sunday-keeping" (I don't like that term) brings the "mark of the beast" is absolutely absurd. It seems that all radical sects brand those who differ with them as those having the mark of the beast. Jehovah's Witnesses say those who do not believe as they do have the mark of the beast. On and on we could go (See Revalation 14:11f for further comments on this point).

Revelation 7:2-4 "And I saw another angel ascend from the sunrising, having the seal of the living God: and he cried with a great voice to the four angels to whom it was given to hurt the earth and the sea, saying, Hurt not the earth, neither the sea, not the trees, till we shall have sealed the servants of our God on their foreheads. And I heard the number of them that were sealed, a hundred and forty and four thousand, sealed out of every tribe of the children of Israel.''

ASSERTION: Sabbath-keeping is the seal, or sign, of God's true people (Exodus 31:17).

ANSWER: The keeping of the sabbath was never referred to as a ''seal'' for anyone, neither the Old Testament Jews nor New Testament Christians! The sabbath was a ''sign'' for the Jews, and them only, but it was never referred to as a seal. Nor is the word ''seal'' ever rendered as ''sign'' in the Bible. Also, if sabbath-keeping be the sign or proof of God's true people since Christ, then all the non-Christian Jews since Christ, even the wicked, would be God's elect, for they all manifested the true sign — sabbath-keeping! I'm sure anyone can see this is patently false and that the proof of a true child of God is not his keeping any such ritual. Now some feel the seal here is the Spirit, which is indeed given as a seal of sonship when one is baptized (in water) into Christ (Acts 2:38; II Corinthians 1:22; Ephesians 1:13; 4:30). Yet, since this text is dealing with those who were already Christians, such is hardly true. Rather, this sealing is borrowed from Ezekiel 9:3f and is symbolic of God's setting apart and sparing from punitive judgment those that are his (cf II Timothy 2:19).

Revelation 11:19 ''And there was opened the temple of God that is in heaven; and there was seen in his temple the ark of the covenant; and there followed lightnings, and voices, and thunders, and an earthquake, and great hail."

ASSERTION: The ark of the covenant, representing the ten commandment covenant, is eternal, being present even in heaven.

ANSWER: Such physical things, including also the temple, have no place in the heavenly realm (Matthew 22:30; John 4:24; Acts 17:24ff; I Corinthians 15:50). The ark of the covenant was presented in the vision to symbolize God's faithfulness in keeping his word and covenants. We need not call to mind the physical ark anymore (Jeremiah 3: 16). There are several other reasons why this verse has nothing to do with what Christians must keep or do:

1. This is symbolic of something in **heaven** and has nothing to do with what Christians must do on **earth**.

2. Shall we also bring back the ceremonial utensils mentioned in chapter five (V.8) and eight (V.3-5), e.g., "altar, censer, incense?" If seeing the ark in heaven means we are to keep the covenant it represented, then seeing these ceremonial objects would mean we are to keep the ceremonial law as well! If not, why not?

3. Symbolic passages such as this are not to be interpreted contrary to other literal passages. Now we have already proven with plain passages that the ten commandments were abrogated with the rest of the old covenant (Romans 7:1ff; II Corinthians 3:6ff; Hebrews 8:6ff); so this passage cannot be interpreted so as to contradict them. It doesn't, either!

Revelation 12:17 "And the dragon waxed wroth with the woman, and went away to make war with the rest (remnant - KJV) of her seed, that keep the commandments of God, and hold the testimony of Jesus."

ASSERTION: The true church — "remnant church" — can be recognized by its keeping the ten commandments.

ANSWER: Everything about the Sabbatarian assertion is inaccurate and full of assumption.

1. A true translation removes their argument for a so-called "remnant church." The word translated "remnant" (KJV) is better rendered "rest" (ASV, NASV, NEB, RSV). The idea is that Satan, via Jewish-Roman persecution, had failed to destroy the church — "the woman"—as a whole (12:6,13-16; cf Matthew 16:18), so he turned his attack upon individual Christians—"the rest of her seed" (12:17; cf I Peter 5:8; Romans 16:20). Thus their theory concerning a so-called remnant church is of their own fabrication.

2. The word "ten" is not before the word "commandments" in this verse. Like always, it is assumed. The New Testament commandments are logically the ones to be understood, for John was concerned with those who held to the "testimony of Jesus" (12:17; cf John 14:15; I Corinthians 14:37; II John 4).

3. This entire context was historically fulfilled in the first century, during the persecution periods of either Nero or Domitian. This book was written primarily to Christians under persecution in John's day, and the prophecies contained in it came to pass soon after his writing (Revelation 1:1,3; 22:10,20 - notice words such as "shortly to come to pass, quickly, at hand"). Thus Revelation twelve has nothing to say about the rise of the Sabbatarian movement — the so-called "remnant church" — centuries later. For several good historical discussions of the book of Revelation, see "The Book of Revelation," Wallace; "Hallelujah Anyway," Richard Rogers; "Revelation", Jim McQuiggan. (See Bibliography).

Revelation 13:11-18 - See 14:11f

Revelation 14:11f "And the smoke of their torment goeth up for ever and ever; and they have no rest day and night, they that worship the beast and his image, and whoso receiveth the mark of his name. Here is the patience of the saints, they that keep the commandments of God, and the faith of Jesus."

ASSERTIONS:

One: All those who keep Sunday show their allegiance to Rome's (the beast) changing of God's ten commandment laws (Daniel 7:25) and have the mark of the beast.

Two: Those who keep the ten commandments do not have the mark (V.12).

ANSWERS:

One: Since we have already proven that Rome (neither the emperor, pope nor church council) had absolutely nothing to do with any such change of God's law concerning the sabbath, then the mark of the beast could not be such (See Daniel 7:25; Revelation 1:10). Also, such an interpretation is contrary to the historical context of the book of Revelation. The mark of the beast was not symbolic of Sunday-keeping but of economic discrimination — "not buy or sell" (Ibid. 13:16f). Christians, in the first century, were financially cut off and boycotted by the Jews and Romans (See 6:5f; cf William Barclay's comments on the trade guilds of that day, discussed at Revelation 2:18-29). This sort of social and economic discrimination preceded the physical persecution brought about by several wicked Roman emperors, e.g., Nero, Domitian, and, later, Diocletian. Thus this mark of the beast would refer to all those who sided with Rome, as the Jews often did (Ibid. 2:9; 3:9), in this persecution and not to those who kept/ keep Sunday instead of Saturday! Let's notice some more errors in this assertion:

1. According to Sabbatarians, all those who keep Sunday vow allegiance to Rome, specifically the Roman church. Yet it is a well known fact that millions keep Sunday and protest the Roman church, calling themselves Protestants!

2. Sunday-keeping is called the cursed mark of the beast by Sabbatarians. Yet what things do Christians do on Sunday to warrant such an ungodly curse? Christians assemble on Sunday, partake of the Lord's Supper, give money for God's work, pray, preach and praise God. Now which one of these things brings the mark of the beast upon him? Who was ever made worse for doing any of these things? What society has been harmed through such practices?

3. Christians can set aside any day, or every day, for special devotion to God and not commit sin (Romans 14:5f; cf Acts 2:42). Thus the Christian's keeping Sunday as a holy day would not be a sinful practice even if he were still obligated to keep the sabbath! Whence then cometh the mark? (Of course, the partaking of the Lord's Supper and the collection for the Lord's work are to be done on the first day of the week - Acts 20:7; I Corinthians 16:1f.)

Two: Again and again Sabbatarians assume what they never have been able to prove, that the word "commandments" means "ten commandments." Such isn't the case here. The commandments are those found in the "faith of Christ" (14:12; cf 12:17; Jude 3).

Revelation 22:14 "Blessed are they that wash their robes (that do his commandments - KJV), that they may have the right to come to the tree of life, and may enter in by the gates into the city."

ASSERTION: Only those who keep the ten commandments have a right to the tree of life.

ANSWER: First of all, they again assume the word "ten" is in the verse when it is not. Secondly, the words "do his commandments" aren't in the more reliable manuscripts and, consequently, in most standard translations (cf ASV, RSV, NASV, NEB). "Wash their robes" is more reliable, especially in light of chapter seven (V.13-17). Any way you look at it the Sabbatarian has no argument!

SUMMATION

1. The sabbath was not kept by anyone before Israel's exodus from Egypt—or for the first 2500 years of man's existence (See Genesis 2:2f; 26:5; Exodus 16:23; 20:8-11; Deuteronomy 5:1-15).
2. The sabbath was never kept by the Gentile nations (See Exodus 23:12; Isaiah 56:6; Acts 13:42-44; cf Job).
3. The sabbath was given only to the nation of Israel (Exodus 16:23-30; 20:1-11; 31:13-17; 34:27f; Deuteronomy 5:1-15; Ezekiel 20:10-12; Hosea 2:11).
4. The sabbath was not given to Israel until after the exodus from Egypt—until Sinai (Exodus 16:23-30; 20:8-11; Deuteronomy 5:1-3, 15; Nehemiah 9:13f; Ezekiel 20:10-12; Hebrews 8:8f).
5. The sabbath was a sign between God and Israel only—no other nation being delivered from bondage by God (Exodus 31:13, 16f; Ezekiel 20:10-12).
6. The sabbath was part of the old Mosaical law which was given only to the nation of Israel (Exodus 20:1-11; Deuteronomy 5:1-15; Nehemiah 9:13f; Psalms 147:19f; II Corinthians 3:6ff; Galatians 4:21-31; Hebrews 8:9f).
7. The sabbath was a part of the old covenant ratified at Sinai and not before (Exodus 24:7f; Hebrews 9:18ff).

8. The sabbath was ceremonial in nature, being classed along with the other Jewish ceremonial days (Leviticus 23:1-8; Numbers 28:9; Colossians 2:16; cf Hebrews 9:1-4).

9. The sabbath was a shadow (thus temporary) of a greater rest (Matthew 11:28ff; Colossians 2:16f; cf Hebrews 4:1-11; Revelation 14:13).

10. The sabbath was not an inherent moral principle to to be kept by all men; it had to be made even for Israel to keep (Exodus 20:8-11; Mark 2:28).

11. The sabbath was abolished with the rest of the old law at the cross (Romans 7:1-6; cf 14:5; II Corinthians 3:6ff; Galatians 3:19ff; cf 4:10; 4:21-31; Ephesians 2:15; Colossians 2:14-17; Hebrews 7:12,18f; 8:6ff; 10:9).

12. Christians are under the new law of Christ and not the old law of Moses (Matthew 17:3-5; John 1:17; cf 7:19; Romans 6:14; 7:1-6; I Corinthians 9:21; II Corinthians 3:6ff; Hebrews 8:6ff; 9:15-17).

13. Christians assemble and worship on a new day—the Lord's day or the first day of the week, Sunday (Acts 2:1ff; 20:7; I Corinthians 16:1f; Revelation 1:10; cf Matthew 28:1, 6, 8ff; Luke 24:13ff; John 20:19,26).

BIBLIOGRAPHY

* Recommended reading

1. Barclay, William, **"The Daily Study Bible"**, All Volumes, The Westminister Press, USA, 1953-60.
2. Barnes, Albert, **"Barnes' Notes on the New Testament"**, One Volume Edition, Kregel Publications, Grand Rapids, Mich., 1970.
3. Berry, George R., **"Interlinear—Greek—English New Testament"**, Zondervan Publishing House, Grand Rapids, Mich., 1973.

*4. Calkins, Erling, **"Why Not Talk to God About the Sabbath?"**, A tract, Box 969, Glendale, Calif.

*5. Canright, D. M., **"Seventh-Day Adventism Renounced"**, Gospel Advocate Co., 1113 8th Ave., So., Nashville Tenn., 1961

6. Clarke, Adam, **"Commentary on the Holy Bible"**, One Volume Edition, Baker Book House, Grand Rapids, Mich., 1967.

7. Dark, Harris J., **"The Sabbath and Seventh Day Adventism Reviewed"**, A tract, Tract Service, P.O. Box 143, Nashville, Tenn.

*8. Douty, Norman F., **"Another Look at Seventh-Day Adventism"**, Baker Book House, Grand Rapids, Mich., 1962.

9. Eusebius, **"Ecclesiastical History"**, Popular Edition, Baker Book House, Grand Rapids, Mich., 1973.

10. Ferguson, Everett, **"Early Christians Speak"**, Sweet Publishing Co., Austin, Texas 1971.

*11. Frost, Gene, **"The $200 Text"**, Firm Foundation Publishing House, Austin, Texas, 1952.

12. Gospel Defender, **"Discussion of the Sabbath"**, Gospel Defender Publishing co., P.O. Box 1941, Decatur, Ala., 1973.

13. Hall, S. H., **"Is the Sabbath of the First Covenant Binding upon Christians Today?"**, A tract, Gospel Advocate Co., Nashville, Tenn.

14. Hoekema, Anthony A., **"The Four Major Cults"**, Wm. B. Erdmans Publishing Co., Grand Rapids, Mich., 1970.

15. Josephus, Whiston's Translation, **Josephus-Complete Works"**, Kregel Publications, Grand Rapids, Mich., 1969.

16. Keil, D.D., and Delitzsch, D. D., **"Commentaries on the Old Testament"**, All Volumes, Wm. B. Erdmans Publishing Co., Grand Rapids, Mich., 1968-69.

17. Lenski, R.C.H., **"The Interpretation of.... all New Testament Letters"**, Augsburg Publishing House, Minneapolis, Minn., 1936-60.

18. Lightfoot, J.B., **"The Apostolic Fathers"**, Baker Book House, Grand Rapids, Mich., 1970.

19. McGuiggan, Jim, **"The Book of Daniel"**, Let the Bible Speak, Inc., 3201 Nth Seventh St., West Monroe, La., 1972.

20. Meredith, Maurice A., **"Dead to the Law"**, A tract, 1815 San Marino St., Oxnard, Calif.

21. Nelson, Thomas & Sons, **"The Holy Bible — ASV"**, Thomas Nelson & Sons, Camden, N.J., 1901.

22. Price, E. B., **"God's Channel of Truth—Is it the Watchtower?**, Pacific Press Publishing Assoc., Mountain View, Calif., 1967.

23. Rogers, Richard, **Hallelujah Anyway,** Discussion of Revelation, Sunset School of Preaching, 34th & Memphis, Lubbock, Tex.

24. Spence, H.D.M. & Exell, Joseph, **"The Pulpit Commentary"**, All Volumes, Wm. B. Erdmans Publishing Co., Grand Rapids, Mich., 1950.

25. Strong, James, **"The Exhaustive Concordance of the**

Bible", Abingdom Press, New York, 1890.

26. Tolle, James M., "**The Sabbath or the Lord's Day—Which?**" Church of Christ, 1226 Glenoaks Blvd., San Fernando, Calif.

27. Wallace, Foy E. Jr., "**The Gospel for Today**", Foy E. Wallace Jr. Publications, P.O. Box 1301, Nashville, Tenn., 1967.

28. Wallace, Foy E. Jr., "**God's Prophetic Word**", Address same, 1960.

29. Wallace, Foy E. Jr., "**The Book of Revelation**", Address same, 1966.

30. White, Ellen G., "**The Desire of Ages**", Pacific Press Publishing Assoc., Mountain View, Calif., 1970.

31. White, Ellen G., "The Great Controversy", Address same, 1971.

32. White, Ellen G., "**Steps to Christ**", Inspiration Books, P.O. Box 8249, Phoenix, Ariz., 1971.

33. Wright, Gerald N., "**There Has Always Been One Baptism**", Star Bible and Tract Corporation, P.O. Box 13125, Fort Worth, Texas, 1975.

34. Wright, Gerald N., "**Perversions and Prejudices of the New World Translation**". Address same, 1975.

35. Wright, Gerald N., "**Second Peter Three—Jewish Calamity or Universal Climax?**" Address same, 1975.

36. Young, Robert, "**Analytical Concordance to the Bible**", Wm. B. Erdmans Publishing Co., Grand Rapids, Mich., 1970.

37. Zondervon, "**The Analytical Greek Lexicon**", Zondervon Publishing House, Grand Rapids, Mich., 1970.

38. Zondervon, "**The Septuagint**", Zondervon Publishing House, Grand Rapids, Mich., 1970.

INDEX

OLD TESTAMENT

Eccles.	12:13	47	Keeping 10 commandments man's whole duty.
Song of Solomon		48	N/A
Isa.	1:13	48	Formalistic sabbath keeping condemned. A list of the holy days.
	2:3	48	New law to go forth from Jerusalem.
	42:21	49	Christ to magnify 10 commandment law.
	56:4-6	50	Supposed prophecy of Gentiles keeping the sabbath.
	58:13	53	Faithful and blessed keep the sabbath.
	66:22f	53	Sabbath supposedly to be kept in heaven.
Jer.	3:16f	55	Good point—ark no longer to be remembered.
	17:21-27	55	Jerusalem to be destroyed if sabbath not kept.
	31:31-34	55	New covenant to be unlike the old.
Lam.	1:7	56	Mistranslation.
	2:6	56	Sabbath no longer kept in Jerusalem.
Ezek.	20:10-12	56	Good points—God giving sabbath to Israel.
	20:13,16, 20-24	57	Israel's breaking sabbath pointed out.
	22:8	57	Israel's profaning sabbath denounced.
	22:26	57	Supposed prophecy of how ministers today profane the sabbath.
	23:38	57	Punishment of Israel for profaning the sabbath.
	44:24	57	Priests to keep sab. in the new sanctuary.
	45:17	58	A list of the holy days.
	46:1,3f,12	58	Worship at the gate on the sabbath.
Dan.	7:25	58	Supposed prophecy of Rome's changing the law and the sabbath.
Hosea	2:11	61	Comment on misuse of this text by opponents. Good point on sabbath being Israel's.
Joel		61	N/A
Amos	8:5-9	61	Comment—misuse by opponents of sabbath.
Obadiah – Zechariah		63	N/A
Malachi	3:6	63	God nor his law ever changes.

NEW TESTAMENT

Reference		Page	
Matt.	5:17-19	63	Christ's fulfilling the law.
	11:28-30	68	Christ is the Christian's sabbath.
	12:1-4	68	Christ's plucking corn on sabbath.
	12:5	68	The sabbath was not kept in the temple.
	12:8	69	Jesus was the lord of the sabbath.
	12:10-12	69	Always lawful to do good on sabbath.
	17:4f	69	Good point, how we hear only Christ.
	19:16-22	70	Eternal life ours only if we keep the Decalogue.
	22:36-40	72	Good point, all the Old Testament hangs on two laws in the ceremonial section.
	24:20	73	Sabbath supposedly still kept in AD 70.
	28:1	76	Saturday and not Sunday is called sabbath.
Mark	1:21	77	Jesus kept sabbath. So must we.
	2:23-28	77	Sabbath is the Lord's day for all men.
	3:2,4	80	Doing good always lawful on the sabbath.
	6:2	81	Jesus kept the sabbath.
	15:42	81	The Preparation day was the day before the sabbath, Friday—Christ's crucifixion day.
	16:1f	81	The disciples rested on the sabbath after Christ's death.
Luke	4:16,31	81	Jesus always kept the sabbath.
	6:1,2,5	81	Jesus is lord of the sabbath.
	6:6f,9	81	Lawful to do good on the sabbath.
	13:10	81	Jesus always kept the sabbath.
	13:14-16	81	Lawful to do good on the sabbath.
	14:1,3,5	81	Lawful to do good on the sabbath.
	23:54	81	The Preparation day before the sabbath.
	23:56	81	Disciples kept sabbath after the cross.
	24:47	83	New covenant from Jerusalem and not Sinai.
John	5:9-18	83	Ridiculous Jewish sabbath regulations.
	5:16,18	83	Jesus persecuted for supposed sabbath violations.
	7:22f	83	Inconsistencies seen in Jewish sabbath regulations.
	9:14,16	83	Christ accused of sinning for healing on sabbath.

II Tim.	2:15	124	Good point on rightly dividing the truth.
	3:15f	125	Profitableness of Old Testament scriptures.
Titus		126	N/A
Heb.	1:1f, 2:2-4	127	Comment on the old and new laws.
	3:11,18	127	Israel not enter God's rest.
	4:1-11	127	Concerning Chritians's sabbath rest.
	7:18f	130	The cancelled-unprofitable law.
	8:6-13	131	The better and different covenant.
	9:1-4	134	Good point on the first covenant being the 10 commandments.
	9:9f	134	Ceremonial duties of the priests.
	9:15-17	135	Ratification of the new covenant.
	10:1	136	The law containing shadows.
	10:9	136	Good point, taking away of first law.
	10:25	136	The approaching day.
	12:18-24	136	Good point on the difference between the old and new covenants.
	13:8	137	Since Jesus never changes, then the law supposedly never changes.
	13:20	138	The eternal covenant.
James	1:25	138	The perfect law of liberty.
	2:8-12	139	The royal law.
I-II Peter		141	N/A
I John	2:3-6	141	To know Christ and walk as Christ one must keep the 10 commandments.
	3:4	142	Sin is transgression of 10 commandment law.
	3:22	143	We must keep the 10 commandments to have our prayers answered.
II-III John		143	N/A
Jude		143	N/A
Rev.	1:10	143	The "Lord's Day"—the 1st. or 7th day?
	7:2-4	151	Seal of saints—sabbath-keeping
	11:19	152	The law of the ark is eternal.
	12:17	153	The so-called "Remnant Church."
	13:11-18	154	Concerning the mark of the beast.
	14:11f	155	Who receives the mark of the beast?
	22:14	156	Those who keep the 10 commandments have a right to the tree of life.

WHEN GOD CHANGED

6 DAYS

CREATION

4000 B.C.

ADAM, NOAH
ABRAHAM
JACOB
JOSEPH

ABRAHAM WAS NOT JUSTIFIED BY LAW
(Rom. 4:1-7)

THE LAW SAID, THOU SHALT NOT COVET
(Rom. 7:7; 13:9; Deut. 7:25; Ex. 20:17; Deut. 5:21)

TEN COMMANDMENTS CALLED "COVENANT"
(Ex. 34:27-28; Deut. 4:12,13; 9:9-11; 1 Kings 8:9-18; 2 Chron. 5:10; 6:11)

THE LAW NOT MADE WITH THE FATHERS BEFORE MOSES
(Neh. 9:14; Deut. 5:1-14)

THE LAW

ONLY ONE LAW IN OLD TESTAMENT
(2 Chron. 31:3; Neh. 8:2,3,8,14,18; Psa. 19:7; Malachi 4:4; Ezra 7:6,12)

EGYPTIAN BONDAGE

ISRAEL DID NOT ENTER INTO GOD'S REST IN CANAAN
(Psalm 94:11; Heb. 3-4)
A FEW ENTERED **(Josh. 22:4)**

RED SEA

"SHADOW"
Gal. 4:10-11; Heb. 4:1-44

2500 YEARS

SINAI
1500 B.C.

1500 YEARS

7th DAY GOD'S REST

HEB. 4:4

NO RECORD OF ANY MAN KEEPING THE SABBATH OR KNOWING OF IT UNTIL MOSES' TIME.

SABBATH MADE KNOWN TO MOSES **(Neh. 9:14)**

SABBATH COMMEMORATED DELIVERANCE FROM EGYPTIAN BONDAGE **(Deut. 5:15; 1 Kings 8:9-21)**

SABBATH A **SIGN** BETWEEN GOD AND ISRAEL (Ezek. 20:10-12)

MEATS
RESTRICTED

NO RECORD OF REGULATIONS REGARDING EATING MEATS.

BEASTS: Chew cud & part hoof **(Lev. 11:1-8)**
FISH: Fins and scales **(9-12)**
BIRDS: (13-19) CREEPING: **(20-23)**

MANY OTHER LAWS: FEAST DAYS, INCENSE, ANIMAL SACRIFICES, REVENGE, CIRCUMCISION, ETC.

PATRIARCHAL AGE

MOSAIC

HIS LAWS

by *Alvin Jennings* 11-30-83

CHRISTIANS STRIVE TO ENTER INTO HEAVEN, GOD'S REST, AFTER THEIR LABORS ARE ENDED (Heb. 3-4)

THE END

SECOND COMING 1 Cor. 15)

"A CHANGE OF THE LAW" (Hebrews 7:12)

IF THE OLD LAW IS NO LONGER IN FORCE, WHAT PURPOSE IS THE OLD TESTAMENT FOR THE CHRISTIAN? **See Romans 15:4 and 1 Corinthians 10:1-10.**

JESUS LIVED UNDER THE LAW OF MOSES AND TAUGHT OTHERS TO OBEY IT **(Matthew 19:18-19; Mark 1:44)**. JESUS "FULFILLED" THIS LAW AND TOOK IT OUT OF THE WAY **(Matthew 5:17-18; Eph. 2:15)**.

THE THIEF ON THE CROSS DIED BEFORE THE LAST WILL AND TESTAMENT OF JESUS WENT INTO FORCE **(Hebrews 9:16-17)**.

CHRIST REMOVED THE FIRST THAT HE MIGHT ESTABLISH THE SECOND **(Heb. 10:9-10)**

TEN COMMANDMENTS ON STONE DONE AWAY, A MINISTRATION OF DEATH **(2 Cor. 3:7-11)**

COVENANT OF THE DECALOGUE ABOLISHED **(Jer. 31:31-34; Zech. 11:10-14; Heb. 8:6-13; 9:15-17)**

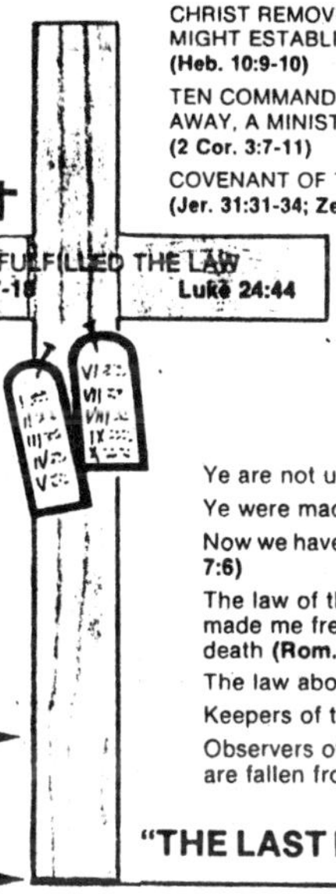

JESUS FULFILLED THE LAW **Matthew 5:17-18** **Luke 24:44**

CHRIST IS THE END OF THE LAW TO THEM THAT BELIEVE (Rom. 10:4)

LAW NAILED TO THE CROSS **(Col. 2:14-17)**, BLOTTED OUT, TAKEN OUT OF THE WAY **(Heb. 8:13)** — A MINISTRATION OF DEATH **(2 Cor. 3:6-11)** "PASSED AWAY."

"LAW OF GOD" and "LAW OF MOSES" TERMS USED INTERCHANGEABLY **(Neh. 8:1,8; Lk. 2:22-23)**

THE LAW GIVEN TILL CHRIST SHOULD COME **(Gal. 3:19-24)**

GRACE

Ye are not under the law **(Rom. 6:14)**

Ye were made dead to the law **(Rom. 7:4)**

Now we have been freed from the law **(Rom. 7:6)**

The law of the Spirit of life in Christ Jesus made me free from the law of sin and of death **(Rom. 8:2)**

The law abolished **(Eph. 2:15)**

Keepers of the law are under a curse **(Gal. 3:10)**

Observers of the law are severed from Christ and are fallen from grace **(Gal. 5:4)**

A NEW AND LIVING WAY **(Heb. 10:20)**

LAW OF LIBERTY **(James 2:12)**

GOSPEL WILL JUDGE US **(Rom. 2:16)**

"THE LAST DAYS" (Acts 2)

JESUS' DEATH 33 A.D.

2000 YEARS + -

SABBATH

1. Commanded To Israel Only — No baking, boiling, travel, work **(Ex. 20:10)**.
2. Examples of Their Observance [Many]
3. Penalty for Violation — Death **(Ex. 31:14-15; Num. 15:32-36)**.

Amos 8:4-9; Hos. 2:11 SABBATH SHALL CEASE WHEN THE SUN GOES DOWN AT NOON.

NO SABBATH:

1. Commanded to Observe
2. Example of Observing
3. Penalty for NOT Observing

NO ONE IS TO BE JUDGED CONCERNING SABBATH KEEPING **(Rom. 14:5; Gal. 4:9-11; Col. 2:14-17)**

CHRISTIANS ASSEMBLE ON THE FIRST DAY OF THE WEEK, THE LORD'S DAY **(Acts 2; Acts 20:7; I Cor. 16:1-2; Rev. 1:10)**

SEVENTH DAY "REVELATIONS" TO ELLEN G. WHITE AND ESTABLISHMENT OF SEVENTH DAY ADVENTIST CHURCH 1843 A.D.

NO FOOD LAW

THRICE REPEATED TO PETER **(Acts 10:9-16)**

NOTHING IS TO BE REJECTED **(1 Tim. 4:1-4)**

DOCTRINES OF DEVILS FORBIDS TO EAT MEAT (FOODS) **(1 Tim. 4:1-4; Col. 2:16)**

(JEWISH) AGE

CHRISTIAN AGE